# AN ALASKAN WOMAN WRITES AGAIN

From the Pipeline, to Field Surveys, to Duct-Tape Cleavage

## Janet McCart

PO Box 221974 Anchorage, Alaska 99522-1974
books@publicationconsultants.com—www.publicationconsultants.com

ISBN 978-1-59433-568-6
eBook ISBN 978-1-59433-569-3
Library of Congress Catalog Card Number: 2015947078

Copyright 2015 Janet McCart
—First Edition—

All rights reserved, including the right of reproduction in any form, or by any mechanical or electronic means including photocopying or recording, or by any information storage or retrieval system, in whole or in part in any form, and in any case not without the written permission of the author and publisher.

Manufactured in the United States of America.

# Other Books By Janet McCart

*Forgiving Rose*
An Alaska Novel of Mystery, Friendship, and Romance

The many-faceted nature of friendship among a group of "forty-something" women is revealed in all its glory and tackiness when the one who struck it rich drowns in her hot tub in Anchorage, Alaska. Forgiving Rose is a novel of mystery, friendship, and romance. Surprising circumstances surrounding the death of a manipulative but endearing friend brings seven women back to Alaska for her funeral, and a most uncommon wake. As old friends reunite, gossip, and relive old times, they find each of them has mixed feelings about their deceased friend, Rose. Details about Rose's hot tub death are revealed as these women connect with the deceased's boyfriend, ex-husband, and stepson. Friendships are tested as ironies unfold, unlikely romances strike—and extravagant surprises await them. When longtime friends hold a wake for Rose, they find that remembering her is easy, but forgiving Rose takes almost more than they can give.

## *I'm Free, I'm Free, I'm Free: Now What?*
## A Semiserious Guide to Early Housekeeping,
## or Things You Wouldn't Let Your Family Tell You

If you've just graduated, or if you haven't—if you're going to advanced school, or if you aren't—if you're setting things in motion to strike out on your own—or if you blew the first or second go at liberty and having your own living space—you're in the right place. If you are serious about rules and guidelines and closets and all the details, go see Martha. If you'd prefer some easy-going, mildly cynical guidance, *I'm Free, I'm Free, I'm Free: Now What?* is for you.

Align the Law of 'what goes up must come down' with the Golden Rule. Now add beds, moving, bills, friends, food poisoning, cleaning, toilets, money, rentals, baseline manners, and roommates, and you have a pretty good idea where we're going here. The bottom line of *I'm Free, I'm Free, I'm Free: Now What?* is to help you become sort-of informed so that you decide, and whatever happens, it's your fault.

*An Alaska Woman Writes Again,* takes the reader along to experience the Trans-Alaska Pipeline, camping in the bush, encounters with bear and moose, and overcoming fear, through much laughter and some tears. These are stories of construction, geological tent camps, fishing, flying, golfing, and other personal stories of self-discovery here are written through the eyes of an Alaskan woman.

# Alaska Map

# Table of Contents

Introduction ..................................................................... 9

1. Trans-Alaska Pipeliner ............................................... 11
2. The Helicopter and the Glacier ................................. 45
3. The Sled Dog and the Momma Bear ........................ 49
4. For the Love of TV in Winter .................................... 55
5. North to Alaska ........................................................... 57
6. Duct Tape Cleavage .................................................... 71
7. Solo on Kepler Lake .................................................... 75
8. Motor Home Reality ................................................... 79
9. Cranberry Moose ......................................................... 87
10. Earthquake Day ......................................................... 91
11. Road Trip from the Top of the World .................... 93
12. Golf Course Flasher ................................................. 111
13. Sears-Roebuck Woman ........................................... 113
14. It's Good to Have Friends ...................................... 123
15. Lime Village Camp .................................................. 131
16. Homer Spit General Store ...................................... 139

# Introduction

I've met many remarkable Alaskan women over many years. These women have stories of bravery, humor, adventure, and truly unique situations far beyond my own. Is this because we find ourselves propelled too far into this place of extremes to back out? To move to Alaska is to move forward, curl up in a ball, or leave.

That leads us to realize many people here (and everywhere) have the ability to be remarkable, and they just don't understand they already are. Maybe that is why we have many humble women out there, with unsurprised smiles, when they watch the antics and actions of the crazy, brave, and adventuresome coming up behind them.

I don't think of myself as a trailblazer, but when I started pulling out journals I saw I was privileged to travel to many once-in-a-lifetime places in Alaska, under uncommon circumstances – much of it occurred before the world stood on its ear with changes of the turn of the century.

> \* Book: *Alaska Women Write*
> With all kinds of experiences a group of Alaska women gathered stories and they were published to surprising success in a book called: *Alaska Women Write*. Because

of complications, the book is no longer in regular circulation. The book dispels the myth that Alaska is a "man's country."

Since this book is no longer on the shelves, it's been suggested to me many times over the years that I put together a book of my stories.

With all kinds of experiences (good, beautiful, and scary), and a sense of humor in mind, I hope you enjoy this book.

Any errors in the story must be blamed on my memory and perception. So please forgive me if you saw it differently. *Please don't think you are obligated to correct me. It's too late*

## 1.

## Trans-Alaska Pipeliner

You, young lady, are going north to Alaska to work at a construction site without a clue as to what or where.

What does that mean? The Trans-Alaska Pipeline was big news, world news at the time, and my uncle had some sway there. My mother had cooked up something with my Uncle to save me from sudden singleness, and angst-filled aimlessness. A trip to who-knows-where Alaska to work. Do what? I'm not a welder. Doesn't matter. Give her something to do.

It was two in the morning when mom called, after we had attended the most depressing wedding ever. (My cousin got married in a baseball jersey. She and her brides' maid were inseparable. The groom and his friends were at a different party.)

With my 2am brain, I said, *"I'll think about it."*

In the middle of the night my mind conjured images of me endlessly pounding on a huge gray pipe with a wrench in the middle of fields of snow. (What else could the job be?) This made the job offer sound like a bad dream and a terrible idea.

The next morning my 25 year old self, my small home-town life, and recent-divorce-brain stared me square in the face. The lack of excitement and meaning in my life was turning me into a dial tone. Everyone was married and having babies. I was in the mood for world travel and adventure, not babies. At this point, pounding a pipe in the Arctic was taking on a certain cachet. I'll do it, whatever it is.

The fact that the pipeline is eight hundred miles long, and routed through some of the most forbidding terrain on earth, did not dampen mother's high spirits in helping me score this job.

I had five days to get my behind from Coeur d'Alene, Idaho, to Anchorage, Alaska. Since everyone thought this was a great idea, it was *not an option* to turn back. The worldly concerns, rental house, furniture, stuff, and job, were falling like dominoes. People were jumping all over the place to help me have this adventure. There, done. Go on your merry way. Wait a minute! Wait a minute!

Determined that I would wear the latest styles in my work on the Trans-Alaska Pipeline, my mom's last chore was to find me stylish clothing. She said, "It never hurts to look your best." Clearly no one told her how they dress on construction sites. There was no turning mother's head with logic.

What did I know?

We came home from a whirlwind shopping tour with rust-colored suede boots, Pendleton woolens, a powder-blue jacket and pantsuit, and two pair of wool slacks with matching blouses and scarves. I splurged on hot pink luggage. It all turned out so that I would be as appropriately dressed as a Candy Striper in a mental ward.

At my going away party, they played a song from John Wayne's movie: *North to Alaska*. Everyone was so excited for my adventure. I had no clue what that would be. With all the fuss, there was no job description, no destination except Alaska, no idea who I'd work with—and no way to turn back.

My seatmate between Seattle and Anchorage was an engineer. "Hang out with the engineers," he coached, peering at me through black-rimmed glasses. He bought me a mini bottle of wine. "They'll take great care of you."

I pictured myself calling: are there any engineers here? Sure. It was my first warning of what a rare bird I would be: a female on the construction site.

The plane dropped through August rain clouds looping over the Alaska Range and the milky Cook Inlet to plunge me into Anchorage, Alaska's largest city. The city of Anchorage surprised me with its skyline of tall buildings, mountains, and abundance of spruce. So much for the igloos and snow.

My uncle's friends retrieved me from the airport. They became my first Alaskan friends. That evening, they took me to dinner at Elevation 92. I'd expected we were going to a down-home cafe. Up-scale, trendy shell-shaped booths faced massive windows that overlooked blue-gray Cook Inlet, and Mt. Susitna, or, as the locals called her, Sleeping Lady. The air in the restaurant fairly buzzed with a famous chef, professional bar tenders, and with business. Money, fifty and hundred dollar bills, lay casually on the table to catch the next round of drinks. Chunky gold nugget watches with jade, gold nugget necklaces (on men and women) with diamonds, and rings were the inclusive, weighty thing. The bigger the nuggets, the cooler the wearer. This was the style I couldn't have planned for.

I was definitely in a foreign country.

So, the next morning, a 6:30 start to a pipeline orientation class seemed to fit with the extreme of it all. If I'd had a clue what I was in for, I wouldn't have come. But it's a little like major surgery, yeah, roll me into the pre-op room. Just go along for the ride. It's better not to know what's to come. You're stuck on the wrong side of the door now.

We found that the next "girls" (versus "boys") orientation wouldn't be held for a week, or more.

"Can you handle class with a room full of guys?" Lee asked.

"No problem. Where's the bathroom?" I'd say that a lot before we were done.

Talk about a candy striper wandering into the mental ward! I only knew that I was going to make three to four times the wages I had been making, and room and board were covered. After that, all was a blank. I would suffer a "boys" orientation among other initiations from the first minute in this world.

Soon, I sat in a classroom with thirty-five men clad in jeans and Carhartts. Many of the guys could barely fill out their paperwork. Half of them wore fabric hats they called *pipefitter caps* made, oddly in my mind, out of calico fabric. Some of these frazzle-bearded guys looked very hung-over, and a long way from home. I'd crossed into the Pipeline Twilight Zone where the ratio ran about 50 men to one woman.

"We are retired Marine drill sergeants," one of the instructors announced with arms crossed and booted feet firmly set. "We have the power to send you home with your tail between your legs."

Great. He was talking to *them*, not *me*. I was special. It turned out not.

"Today, over the next six hours," the other Marine drill sergeant shouted, "you will learn about environmental safety, personal safety, Arctic safety, health," he paused and glanced at me, "and, sexually transmitted diseases, and hygiene."

All eyes landed on me. I was recently divorced and unused to being treated as if I was interesting. I attempted to suppress a flowery blush. The class language, projector slides, film, and photos must have been vintage Marine boot camp. Some of the slides showed more than I ever wanted to learn about what frostbite and sexually transmitted disease could do to human tissue.

Many of the guys were more entertained by watching me, hoping I'd faint or something, than attending to the class. But I was of the new school. No crying. No running. No fear…

We heard about the dangers of metals fracturing, and oil becoming solid at forty below zero. We heard about cabin fever, which was a kind way of saying that someone who had cabin fever had *lost their head*. Next, rabid fox. Don't feed the animals. Then there was the danger of drinking alcohol that had sat out all night in those below zero temperatures. What? It seemed some of the operators hid the vodka bottle under the seat of their behemoth. Imagine tipping that colder than ice fluid first thing in the morning. Frostbite of the mouth, esophagus, and stomach. In other words, no drinking on the job. (How cold was it going to be out there? My cute ski jacket was not looking so great.)

We saw instructional tapes about how to deal with black bears, brown bears, polar bears, eagles, fox, and moose. The basic message was: stay away unless you'd like bodily harm and/or rabies. This somehow led into the topic of bathing. We were instructed to take baths/showers daily. Okay then. (We had to be told to do that!)

Class intimidation done, we were corralled with our luggage, and loaded onto vans. It turned out it was a *strike one* on the record to call *luggage* anything but *gear*. *Ha-ha, she called it luggage.* I was going to learn a lot of new words for things. The old words were subject to ridicule. Like, it was okay for a batch of guys to advance and say to another guy: how are you, you old coon-ass? I braced for a rumble, but it was hugs all around.

I didn't know filthy vans could go that fast on mud and potholed roads. We were packed so tight in the van that it was like riding an earthquake with strangers in your lap.

Next stop: medical offices and physicals. As I stood in a little cubicle changing into a short paper robe so I could join in a line-style physical with over a dozen men, panic set in. This was carrying the integration-thing a little too far! I wasn't giving up my underwear.

A pipefitter said, "Can't you take this little girly someplace else? She might decide to make a pass at me." A nurse pulled me out of the fidgeting group of men. I was so disoriented I had failed to ask for my own exam. Grateful, I followed the nurse, dragging my new title, *girly (emphasis on the g)*. Somehow it didn't sound endearing.

After the physical, hearing test, vision test, spinal exam, and blood work, we were packed in a too familiar way in vans, (seat belts, ha!), and once again sent careening—this time, to the Anchorage International Airport.

Sandwiches, cookies, brownies, donuts, coffee, tea and bananas had been available all day. Anxiety was growing, not ebbing. My reaction to extreme anxiety is nausea. I couldn't even picture what would be next on the agenda. I needed chicken-noodle soup and a nap. Try and get that on Planet Pipeline.

Our bags were dumped out of the back of the van in a heap at the Anchorage International Airport. We peeled ourselves apart and went to collect our gear. There, another drill sergeant announced: "You will be going to one of four destinations: Prudhoe Bay, Cold Foot, Pump Station Eight, or Valdez."

My name was called as part of the Valdez contingent, pronounced Val-deez. (*Strike two* is saying Val-dez versus Val-deez.) Nine of us traipsed through the airport, not to the jet flight terminals, but down long and grubby hallway, carrying our loads, where we were then packed onto a mini ten-seat plane.

The weather, as we climbed the tin stairs to the little plane, was gray, windy, and foul. There were five small vinyl seats on either side of the ten-inch wide aisle. Our gear bulged from the back.

"Where's the rest room?" I asked a teenager who turned out to be the pilot.

He pointed to a tin coffee can on the floor. Then he asked, "How much do you weigh?" Uh…

This was to be a question asked every time a person got on anything less than a full size jet. The pilots had to calculate the weight of us and our bags so that the plane was not overloaded or unbalanced. Not a good time to lie.

Great. This toy plane was supposed to carry us, and our luggage, over Cook Inlet, the North Pacific, the Chugach Range, and the

Kenai Peninsula and it mattered how much we weighed! A rough hour ride if all went well, and the weather guaranteed it wouldn't. I hadn't been away from a bathroom for longer than thirty minutes in two days. The herd mentality kept me moving forward. The twin engines were so noisy that conversation was impossible. If I were going to chat nervously, I would be talking to myself.

This was nothing like flying in a jet. I felt as if I was being rolled, helplessly, by Mother Nature's rough hand. My pink Samsonite luggage glared through the other duffle bags. If there was heat in the plane it didn't reach me. The plane took off and immediately started bouncing on the wind. Nobody laughed. I started praying. At one point, the teen pilots took out a map. Given our ability to see absolutely nothing but white, fear surpassed nausea. One series of bounces threw all our carry-ons to the back of the plane, clobbering us and the would-be rest room. The next bump knocked the gear in our direction.

At one point the pilots decided to fly below the clouds, which had us very near the water. Finally, after a cold, humid, and bumpy hour-plus ride, the pilot said, "We're gonna slam-dunk this baby down onto the runway. Hang on." No kidding. "Slam-dunk."

I could spy, between clouds, a little black ribbon that was apparently the airstrip. I didn't know this tarmac was surrounded by mountains like a basketball hoop. We were *slam-dunked* and delivered to the airplane terminal at Valdez, frazzled, but alive.

Since the saw-toothed mountains were mostly veiled in mist, my first impression of Valdez was: mud. There was mud everywhere. The terminal was surprisingly modern, had five air service companies, and was full of people backed-up, waiting to catch a plane out. A driver found us, and told us ours was the only plane to make it in to Valdez during the whole day. Yeah. We had all been shaken, stirred, and dumped out in Valdez, Alaska. All faces were pale, one guy had gotten sick, and one of my fellow travelers knelt and kissed the ground.

Our guide pointed us to his mud-covered van, and indicated our bags (GEAR!) should go in the back. At this point all of us were getting awfully tired of being herded, packed, and prodded. Even these workers-to-be, who looked like they might have bucked airport suitcases for a living, were getting pretty weary of lugging enough gear to live on to and from various buildings and assorted vans and a plane.

The van driver had taken lessons from the drivers in Anchorage. On the trip to the Terminal Camp, we saw a lot of mud and felt a lot of potholes and got too familiar with one-another. The ride seemed much longer than 45 minutes.

It was mid-evening when we were dropped off outside the Induction Center at the Valdez main camp. It would have broken my spirit if I had known this was only the *beginning* of my odyssey.

It would be a week before I would see that Valdez was a booming frontier alpine town, nestled at the base of steep mountains, on Prince William Sound.

Ankle deep mud nearly flooded my beautiful boots as we were dumped out in front of a square, yellow and white tin building. Inside, a large, block-shaped woman shouted rapid-fire, "Stand in line at the arrows on the floor and listen up." (She really said "listen up.") "No drugs, no booze, no ladies of the evening in your rooms. We recommend you take a shower at least every other day. Meals are served morning and night at both of the two-thousand-man mess halls. You take your lunch with you from the mess hall. Security will check your badges everywhere you go. Craft people must get brass and check through the Brass Shacks coming and going from the job."

As I was contemplating what brass was, and why the craftspeople needed to check it, she frowned at me and pointed. "You, get last in line." What did I do?

I watched as she took badge pictures, gave out our new identification (to be worn at all times), stamped out strange little brass discs, and gave out room keys to the various barracks, (barracks?) to the eight guys in front of me and sent them on their way. There wasn't much conversation going on. I figure we were all a bit overwhelmed.

Then she came to me.

"What's brass?" I asked, hoping to soften her a bit, maybe make a friend.

She eyed me, rolled her eyes, and sighed. "It's a number identifying the hourly craft guys. Brass is used to clock in and clock out."

Yeah, now I knew what it was... And, unbeknownst to me, I'd identified myself as a *political hire*. No one wanted a *political hire*. I already knew that.

She flipped huge barracks' room charts back and forth slapping them down. "I don't have room for another woman in this camp."

Was I supposed to sleep in the mud? I tried to look sympathetic as she complained loudly about having more people than beds.

Finally she said, "You'll have to go back over to Keystone Camp, *girly*."

"Where's that?"

"It's a big flat ugly space by the airport."

"I just came from there..."

She didn't care. With that, she did my paperwork, and shoved me in front of a colored sheet to take my photo. What is a Keystone Camp? I figured it's a long mud-and-pot-hole ride back to barracks by the airport. My picture looked as if I'd been drained of blood by a vampire. It would be around my neck for a year and a half.

"Okay, girly," she said, "Next you go across the road and get your hard hat at that shack over there." She pointed through a muddy window. Huge buses splashed and wallowed by in a steady stream.

"I don't think I'll need one of those," I ventured.

"Honey," she snapped, "you're on a construction site now. Wake up and smell the coffee. Get your damn hard hat, or go home."

Did I really look like a girly? By this time, my blush was worn out. I wanted to smack her but I didn't have the energy, and, some-

19

thing told me if there was a fight she'd win. Off I went to get my hard hat. I was a walking example of a *political hire*, I didn't come through a union or personnel, (*strike three*), and therefore a gross burden to be borne rudely and impatiently on a construction site.

Crossing the road sounded like such a simple order. Yet, by the time I got my room assignment and badge, rounded up my two pieces of pink Samsonite, tucked in my plaid wool Bobby Brooks' pants, and strapped on a carry bag and purse I realized I had been abandoned. My van mates had all disappeared. I felt like a lonely pack mule dodging busses.

Finally, a bus stopped to let me pass through the mud-lake they called a road, and I got my last piece of gear—the hard hat with my name on it. It sat high on my head like a chicken looking for a place to roost. I balanced it on my rain-wet head, slung my purse on one shoulder, my shoulder bag on the other, and grabbed my two suitcases yet again and crossed the road.

Now what? A bus stopped to tell me I couldn't get on the Keystone bus with luggage. Um, how was I supposed to get to this Keystone place? I was getting more than my share of stupid cat-calls from passing buses. I was afraid the beastly woman at the induction center would send me home if I asked how to get to my barracks (?) again. So, instead, I stood in the mud, and waited for the inspiration. Rain poured on me, and my hateful pink suitcases. The torrent ran off my hardhat and down my back.

After some time, a young, dark-haired fellow in a muddy workvan drove up. He stepped out of the truck, tipped his hard hat to me, and went inside. When he came back out, he paused before climbing into his truck. "Why are you standing in the rain?"

"I'm supposed to go to Keystone Camp, and I don't know how. The bus won't let me on."

"Can't have luggage on the buses. Carrying stuff is a Laborers' job. I'm not supposed to do this with the union agreements and all," he said as he loaded my suitcases in his truck, "but I don't know how you are supposed to get there either."

He drove me over to Keystone Camp, next to the airport, where we had been *slam-dunked* earlier that evening. He helped me carry my bags into the Rec center. Inside the door, a tall woman, in tight western jeans, stood surrounded by admiring men. The Camp Coordinator, she surveyed me and my stuff. She flashed me a quick don't-latch-on-to-me smile, and welcomed me to the camp. She was all business and soon she had rounded up a key for my room and mailbox, and gave me a gray wool blanket. "You go over two buildings, down four, and across three and make a left." I think that's what she said. I nodded, rounded up my belongings, and went out the door.

A sea of yellow and white tin buildings swimming in pouring rain stood in front of me. I walked a few feet and plopped my bags in the mud. There looked to be 20 or 30 buildings. My mind went blank and my hands and shoulders shook with luggage fatigue. (I think *luggage* is the appropriate name for pink Samsonite, not *gear*.) My hands refused to carry those bags one more foot, my brain shut down. Like a blessing, another nice man took pity on me and helped me get my load to the women's barracks.

By barracks, I mean square, aluminum-sided, modular ATCO trailers, set-up to form a single-story block of rooms surrounding the laundry, shower, and toilet facilities. The building smelled like industrial cleaner, wet carpet, boots, and wet wool. The halls were floored with gray, worn linoleum; the rooms had paisley-orange indoor-outdoor carpets. Each room held twin beds separated by a small, battered desk. In the tiny space at the end of each bed was a closet that wouldn't hold my luggage. Gold vinyl curtains hung in the small windows. (This look was never good.) My bedroom walls were lined with dark paneling that was so thin I could hear someone breathing in the next room. The beds each sported white sheets and one gray wool blanket.

I dumped my gear and wandered to the center of the structure. The laundry room, and the bathroom were in use, but it looked to me as if there were at best a dozen women in the whole place. I gazed in dismay at shower curtains that did not cover the shower, toilets stalls like those used in gas stations, and a row of rust-stained sinks that provided zero privacy. A shower would have to wait until morning.

I wound my way back to my room. Suddenly it occurred to me that I had no idea where to get food, how to get back over to the main camp of five thousand people in the morning, where to go once I got there, or anything else. At least I had a bathroom. I sat draped over my luggage trying to get the energy to unpack.

A woman wearing dirty overalls, knee-high rubber boots, and a hard-hat stomped into the barracks and stopped at the sight of me, hanging over my luggage.

She paused at my door. "What's the matter kid?" (Was it that obvious?)

I took a deep breath and told her all the things I *didn't* know about my slot in Valdez. Which was everything.

She listened, sized me up, and said, "It's Valdez, with a hard e."

"Oh, yeah, I forgot," I was already tired of Valdez with a hard e.

She shook her head, and managed to look good in green rubber boots and a grubby yellow slicker. "Okay. The mess hall is just two blocks in front of us, but it's about to close. The Rec Hall is about three rows back, and you get your mail, and some snacks there. I don't think you're with craft. What do you do?" she asked, eyeing my clothes.

"Office type stuff, typing, filing, transcription..."

She nodded as if it was clear I wasn't part of the labor force and I must be a *political hire*, and like the rest, I wouldn't make it three days. But she took pity. "Remember this. There are two categories of workers on the construction site, they are *Staff* and *Craft*. Staff jobs are stuff like management, admin, personnel, quality control, engineering, and hourly office support—pretty much non-union. Craft jobs are the pipefitters, electricians, laborers, Teamsters, iron workers—mostly union."

For some reason *that* made sense.

She continued. "You need to catch the Staff bus at five-thirty in the morning. It's marked on the end of the second row. That should get you to the right places. You okay now?"

I nodded, pushing back the urge to follow her.

She strolled down the hall to her room. I swear, from somewhere in the barracks I heard the song: *Welcome to the Hotel California; you can check out, but you can never leave.*

The mess hall was closed, so I pulled a few crumpled packs of crackers from my purse. I didn't sleep much, anxious about nearly everything I could think of, including getting up on time and group-showering with the girls.

If the umpteen diesel buses gunning and idling nearby, and the women banging through the tin showers, and the cassette players blasting hadn't awakened me, I would have been in a coma. Except, I didn't think a little coma would be considered a good excuse for missing work here.

The women seemed to be on zombie-auto-pilot as they showered, brushed teeth, blew dry, and used the rest rooms. This provided its own sort of privacy. The women were laborers and heavy equipment operators. One gal's bra, draped over the shower, was a startling dark gray at a time when they only came in white. (That night she would dawn a mini-skirt and silk blouse to go on a date. After a 12 hour work day!)

Everyone seemed blind to anything but their own business and my questions got one word answers. I chose my cute powder-blue pantsuit with matching scarf. My soft blue jacket had dried out on the radiator, and because I had no others, I put my damp suede boots back on. I marched, hard-hat in hand, to the mess hall. I had to have more crackers, maybe tea and some fruit.

I didn't realize that there were only ten women in this four-hundred-fifty-man camp, and that the others were dressed in overalls. I stepped in the door of the massive mess hall that was set up cafeteria style, with oversized picnic tables provided eating spaces. The whole place soon went silent. Every face took in me and my powder-blue. This was not a powder-blue kind of place. I stood stuck like a deer in the headlights, considering whether I should flee and go another day without food, or endure this overwhelming circus-level attention.

Obviously, they didn't get much entertainment here. The need for food won, but barely. As hundreds of eyes bore down on me, I flushed red to my toes and swiftly found the lunch items, threw a sandwich, crackers, milk, and some fruit in a bag. There was a mouse running around and around in the box of bananas which caused me to be cautious of the fruit boxes forever more. I left.

Outside, rain poured down as I wound my way through a maze of buses with my helmet pitched on my head. The combined smell of mess-hall bacon, diesel, and wet wool is imprinted on my brain permanently from those mornings. The thing that continued to drive me was that I didn't have any choice but to go forward. There was no *back*.

Finally, I found the bus marked "staff" and climbed on board to sit in the first seat behind the bus driver's. This was one of many mistakes I was to make this day.

I sat on the empty bus and waited. Fumes from the diesel buses mixed with the strong aroma of tuna and onions in my unfortunate choice of sandwich. I felt pretty certain that it would have been difficult to pick a smell better calculated to turn my nervous stomach. As I was struggling with a good location for the stinking lunch, I was tapped firmly on the shoulder by a bearded, Carhartt-clad man. "That's Tiny's seat," he said. He was serious. "Since you're a *girly* and since he's sick, you can sit there today."

"Are you sure?" I asked.

He wasn't.

"You can have this seat back here as yours," a slight man with a beard hollered.

I made my way back and sat next to him on the aisle. "It takes seniority to get window seats," he explained. "They're the best for leaning against to sleep."

Sleep, here?! I looked around and heads with caps were leaned against the windows, eyes were shut. I was to learn it was a good use of time—that or look at mud for the long ride. I never mastered sleeping on the bus.

Soon, the curiosity of a woman had almost everyone on the bus intent on helping me find my place of work and welcoming me to Valdez (with a long e). I was now famous for my pink bags and powder blue pants suit. I was getting a lot of friendly hard-timing and guidance I was reluctant to trust. So I told the fellow next to me about the woman yelling at me at the induction center. "She made me go get this helmet," I declared, holding out my hard-hat-cum-lunch-container.

"HELMET!" he grabbed it, holding it out of my reach. "Did you hear that everybody? She called this a HELMET! I guess we must be in a war zone." Ha-ha-ha. We had quite a jolly ride.

"Kick me in the leg," he said.

"No, that's okay." I smiled back, wondering if he was crazy. It was possible to seriously question the reality of this muddy-tube of the bus, and wonder where it was going. Had we crossed into another dimension? How long could this ride be?

"Come on, kick me," he said. He poked and teased until I finally kicked him. His leg was aluminum. This was apparently very entertaining to everyone who was awake.

The staffers on the bus, mostly QC (quality control) guys, bid me farewell at one of dozens of yellow and white ATCO aluminum buildings. It turned out to be the right one.

The administration building was configured in eight double-trailers end-on-end—this was one banana of a building. I climbed off the bus into the mud and looked around me. There was heavy equipment, loud back-up beepers, what I guessed to be the brass shacks, ACCO trailers like tinker toys, storage buildings, flood lights, muddy boots, important people in hard hats walking quickly, and mucky pick-ups. I walked up the wide snow-and-mud-grill steps to double doors that looked official. I finally wandered and questioned my way to my new workplace, and my new boss.

The administration manager was from Texas. His skin was the color of yellow sealing wax, and he looked like he deeply regretted signing on for this one last job before retirement, or death. Whichever came first.

"Great, another *@#! *political hire*," he proclaimed to the heavens. I was already a pariah. "What am I supposed to do with her? I don't need another dead weight. Why didn't anyone *#*! tell me she was coming!?" He slammed things around his dark office and desk.

Then to me he said, as if hope were futile, "Please tell me that you at least have a few #@*#@ office skills. The last *political hire* was so bad I sat her down with a typewriter and a ream of paper and told her to type something and throw it in the trash." (This would have been ideal for a novelist.)

I quickly came to understand that being stuck with a *political hire* label, in most cases, was considered to be about as desirable catching a sexually transmitted disease. I was finally rattled with fatigue and confusion and lack of food, but was not about to let him know it. "I have all the office skills you could ask for. I'm good."

He grunted, shoved himself out of his chair, and barked at me. "What have you got that hardhat stuck on your silly head for? Do you think the roof's gonna cave in? You'll be lucky to make it a week, girly." With that, he went down the hall yelling. At this point I drooped into a chair like a wet bag full of sand named Girly.

His secretary came to my rescue. "Don't worry about him, he's always that way. You look sick," she stated. "For heaven's sake, get rid of this thing!" She pinched my tuna and onion sandwich from the bag and removed it from the room. She came back to her desk, sat down, and stared at me. "Your face is green."

"I'm okay," I mumbled, "just point me to the bathroom."

When I came back, Ross had hot tea with a little sugar, and a pile of soda crackers waiting for me. I latched onto her like a duckling fresh from its shell. I'd met my first pipeline friend, Ross.

I sat, watching her do her work, catching hallway conversations, making several trips to the bathroom, and eyeing the clock. These unproductive hours going by couldn't be good. I'd never sat idle at a job in my life.

By late afternoon, after a lot more swearing and people wondering what to do with me, I had my new job on staff. I was delivered to a long conference room, with an impossibly long conference table. It was stacked with enumerable bankers boxes full of paper. There were stacks of paper piled on and under the table, and up wall. I looked at the front of the boxes—Greek. Topics: *West Tank Farm Biological and Ecological Study, Drafts. Pipeline Operating agreements among W, X, Y, and Z, at the Valdez Terminal Site—Drafts.* Amended operating agreements. Phone-book size labor agreements. Personnel files. Soil testing. *Environmental Study of Flotation Docks A, B, C, in Conjunction With the Department of Environmental Services, USA—Drafts...*

"File these by the Dewey Decimal Filing System," ordered a pock-faced man dressed entirely in black. He waved grandly around that sorry room like he'd showed me what happens to folk who turn up as a political hire without papers. "Here's your job, girly..." There was a clock. I thought it was broken. But, no.

My skills didn't include the Dewey Decimal Filing System. But I acted like I knew what to do.

Commando-man laughed and walked out. I dumped my stuff and made a thorough inspection of the place. I stopped counting at 60 boxes. I pushed through stacks of paper, and opened boxes in a quest for Dewey and his Decimal System. Luckily, all the papers had little numbers in the right corner, so I started putting them in order, which was accidentally right.

Ross seemed to understand the Dewey Decimal System enough to say she thought I had it right, and checked in on me

27

briefly, but no one on the construction site seemed interested in getting involved with me or these records. They made it clear they were sorry for me, but not available as help. People stopped by to introduce themselves. "Pace yourself," they all said. "We have long days, and you need to pace yourself." I'd never been on a job where I was advised to *pace myself*, to do less than going flat out. Was this a little initiation trick? I plowed into the sea of papers and started making piles. At least it looked like I was accomplishing something. I'd never seen a clock move more slowly. I was to be in this shoebox room full of boxes of files for twelve hours a day. It's one of those times when it's better not to think. Just look like you're thinking. Pick up another piece of paper.

Ross took me to one of the Valdez Terminal Camp mess halls that night for dinner. It was built to handle two thousand men. The room steamed with well wrapped brown and gray men, and wet clothes. Every sort of face fur was present. The workers lined up in their drab pipeline gear and marched forward to choices of meat, potatoes, rice, gravy, vegetables, and the like. Desert was in a side area. The fare was heavy and caloric.

My clothing was still garnering a lot of attention, but now I had Ross to guide me and I wasn't alone. Later she showed me the bus schedule and sent me on my way back to Keystone Camp.

A cat-box like smell permeated the bus, and I was passed a cigarette—my first look at pot. I passed it on without a try. It might have helped if I had tried it. We had a jolly old ride back to the Airport Camp. I was able to find my barracks as it was the one right next to the busses that ran 24 hours a day. (The smell of diesel is burned on to my brain.) As it turned out, until I got on my feet, I ate with Ross at the main camp mess hall.

As I started my fourth day, and shredded my finger on yet another paper edge, I allowed myself to come out of shock, and really ponder this work schedule. I would be filing six or seven days a week, twelve hours a day, with thirty minutes for lunch. Further, I would commute from another camp on a bus traveling forty minutes each way. I would have to face down hundreds of guys to get my meals. I would have to inhale diesel fumes and hear back-up-beep-beep-beeps morning and night.

I'd settled into my barracks room, and learned to get some sleep despite the commotion. Then I got a roommate. My new roommate, a hot-tempered redhead, added charm to the deal by sitting up at two every morning to smoke an unfiltered Pall Mall, in rhythm with the surging busses. She went back to sleep while I considered putting a pillow firmly over her head. It was then I knew I was seriously stuck in the outback of hell. I grabbed my extra gray wool blanket possessively, I was the only one who had two, and lying next to those tin walls was cold business.

There was no way I could yell *uncle*—stop this crazy ride - because my uncle had stuck his neck out to get me this job. My family would be forever shamed if I didn't stick it out. Giving up was not an alternative. I was propelled day by day by the possibility of family disgrace (which was not to be born in those years) and the momentum of the days. With overtime I was making four times my old salary. So, I hunkered down. Day after day I told myself, just one more day.

Fortunately, after two weeks (I was getting to be an old hand, turnover was so high), my uncle came to see me and the general manager of the Valdez Terminal. Suddenly, I was getting hugs. A woman in personnel got mad at her boyfriend and drug-up. (*Dragging-up* was pipeline lingo for quitting, versus a case of the *red-ass*, which describes exactly how the person feels just before he or she drags up.)

With my uncle's arrival and good friendship with the site manager, and with other woman's departure, I had a job sitting next to my new friend, doing personnel work which I found a lot more entertaining than miles of filing. People stopped calling me a *political hire* in case I had some pull. (Those awful files and the file room were never touched again while I was there.) My boss stopped swearing at me so much.

Getting through the first weeks was an endurance initiation. I learned the value of *pacing one's self*. I later found out that six out of seven people drug-up before spending one or two weeks on the site. The strangeness, the long hours at a desk or laboring on the job around the site, the darkness and rain, and the uncommon work, politics, and after-work life kept things challenging.

When Ross figured I was going to hang in there, she took me to Valdez proper to shop for normal clothes—jeans, mud boots, raincoat, flannel shirts and the like. The powder blue Pendleton and swede boots were just not working. They got packed up and sent home. Pea-green rubber boots were a necessity. The climate in Valdez is northern rainforest with record setting rains and snows, fogs and coastal misting. It never got the super-cold of the northern part of the state. But it snowed two and three feet or more in a day, and pothole lakes in the snow taught a person to pay attention to where they put their feet.

Ross also took me to the bank where I opened my Alaska account. Friday evening at the bank was a gladiator event. Every teller-window was open. Big, brown Carhartt-garbed workers in bunny boots lined up and out the doors as tellers loudly counted out the amount each person took in cash. There was no auto deposit—or privacy. "Two thousand one hundred, three thousand one hundred." (That was a lot of money then.) We listened to their totals, figuring who had the biggest check of the week. It was generally a pipefitter/calibrator. Our checks, as clerical workers, were the lowest on the site.

My new boss recommended it, so I made the choice to work six days a week and take off Sunday. That meant that on Sunday I was restless and walked around the flat land near the airport.

I wasn't familiar with the bus schedule so I decided to walk from Keystone Camp to town. I got several miles out with no town in site. I turned around to head back and a guy pulled up on a motorcycle and asked me if I wanted a ride back to camp. It was now raining, and yes I did. It seemed farther than five miles back. I had no illusions about arriving with my hair gracefully blown. I had a skunk strip of mud up my back, and my hair was sopping wet. But, the ride was as it must be, intimate, and I hung on for dear life. But there's something that makes one smile upon riding a motorcycle.

On Sunday I joined the pool or card games in the rec center with others who had chosen to take Sunday off. (We were the ones who were able to stick it out.) (Besides, a person has to do laundry and sleep once a week.) I made a group of new friends—pipefitters and electrical engineers. We had our own dining table (an oversized, traditional wood picnic table) and met up at breakfast and dinner for some homey conversation. These times rolled with military-barracks-like bonhomie. We all spoke the same pipeline language, lived the same stress and weirdness, and shared jokes and outrageous work stories: guys who slept under a bench all day; bears breaking in anyplace for food, climbing stairs, and tearing up metal desks and being good camera fodder; a well-liked man was killed by ice falling on the roof of his truck from one of the unfinished tanks… Of course, there was always news of someone who with no warning got mad and drug-up.

The table evolved with new hires filling in behind, and those who *got mad and drug up*. Getting mad about some perceived injustice was the only justification for quitting a job with such crazy-good wages. Everything was exaggerated and intense in this strange world, including injustice and loneliness.

My family sent me a box with homey items for my room: an orange and brown crocheted comforter, a clock radio, more appropriate underwear and socks, and special foods. It did help.

After some time the work started the early winding down, and they closed the Keystone Camp and moved us over to the Valdez Terminal Camp. The ATCO trailers were a little newer there, and the buildings stair-stepped up—fifteen buildings up in three rows, spaced on a fairly steep mountain incline. We now had gold carpet. Our units were now stretched out down a single hall per floor (two floors), with the bathroom, showers, toilets, and clothes washers located in the center. It was never quiet. People stomped up and down the stairs and the tin hallways, smoked pot and laughed, or drank alcohol and argued—or snored. The doors had automatic locks on them so if a sleepy person dashed to the bathroom in the middle of the night without remembering their key, there was no one in the building to get the master key. For those who went nude, this was a particularly uncomfortable situation which occurred too often.

The heat vents carried conversations, music, and TV sounds, far and wide. It was here that I learned to use ear plugs. I can still twist those pieces of foam in and block out major amounts of noise. They were a construction site necessity.

My first barracks at the terminal site had me as the only female in a 24 room floor of the barracks. The first night I went to take a shower I heard a stampede and voices saying, "She's in the shower! She's in the shower!" What? I was the only "she!" Dread and the stomping in my direction hit me like a punch. My brain went blank. They couldn't be talking about me.

Fortunately I was well robed and wrapped as about six of them arrived at my shower stall. I stood there speechless. I heard another stampede and came to the conclusion that this was going to be really bad. Then I saw my table-mates who had heard what was going on. While the two groups confronted each other, I scuttled down the hall to sound of shouting. I have no idea how my guys found out. I'd never had any problem this way in all my time at camp, and was stunned, and incredibly grateful to my friends. As long as I had that room I went down the hill to a mixed barracks to shower, and did my morning routine in the laundry-room sink.

My boss helped me get a *towner* for a roommate in a mixed male and female barracks. (They'd pretty much given up trying to keep barracks all male or all female.) A *towner* was a person who lived in town but kept camp status in order to eat in the mess-halls. So, I had a coveted room to myself. As friends drug up, I was left with a TV (one station that played Kojak and Saturday Night Live). I had a TV, microwave, a mini refrigerator, and a popcorn popper. I had a nice cassette player, two tiny closets, and a double bed, and night table. What else could a person need?

I settled in for the long run with an actual bedspread, throw pillows, décor, and full length mirror. When leading tours of the site they often used my room as an example. A female friend, Olga, was able to get the room next door to me. We could talk to each other from our beds in normal voices and hear the other easily. She and I both stayed in camp to the end.

We went through the seasons while in Valdez. Summer had the sun barely going down, and the world was a green kingdom supplying raspberries and salmon berries, and to a person with a fishing pole, a beautiful silver salmon.

You don't think that those good old boy oil workers from the south were going pass a summer without a barbeque grill! The welders made fancy set-ups from scrap parts. Salmon was such a welcome break from routine chow-hall food.

One afternoon, while delivering mail to the mess hall, I'd stepped through the double doors to find myself stuck with a massive brown bear in the arctic entry (small room, four doors). The bears weren't aggressive with all the dumpster food. I ran out unharmed but still alarmed, leaving the door open when I left so the bear wouldn't surprise anyone else.

Bug dope was a necessity. I kept a man's flannel shirt doused with bug spray, never washed it, and always wore it as a repellant outside during spring-summer-fall mosquito seasons. I kept a doused ball cap for the same reason. People often tried to catch extra-large mosquitoes with clear tape in order to be able to press and present the proof of the size of these suckers. The weather was kind to mosquitoes in Valdez, and they proliferated.

Friday night was steak night, so the rec hall was skipped in preference of the mess hall, where most guys took at least two steaks. (They weren't *that* good.) Food incidents were a favorite topic. A piece of glove in the lasagna, a mouse in the fruit boxes, a bolt in the meatloaf. One night while eating pasta I bit down on a big spiral of metal from the industrial can openers. Yuck. Although considering the volume of food that went through those halls, these incidents were surprisingly few.

On occasional Saturday nights a few of us gals went to town and ate dinner at one of several good restaurants. The town was booming and could support chefs from around the country. When we'd ask for our check, we were surprised that someone there had already paid our bill. As time went on, that happened every time we went out. We all wondered why. I'm guessing it was loneliness, kind hearts, and good wages. It was humbling every time.

After our non-mess-hall dinner, we would sometimes go to one of several clubs and dance to bands from Vegas. Females never sat out a song, and never bought a drink. That cuts both ways. We were always aware of the unfair odds. Having seven or ten drinks bought for one, lined up on the table, with endless dance partners—it wasn't as enviable as it may sound to some. To others, it was terrifying. Hundreds of dollars would lay on the tables and while people continued buying rounds. Cocaine and pot were easily had if one had the inclination. One of the favored songs of the time was: *driving my train high on cocaine...* The song was more popular than the drug. Energy was so high, time lost all meaning on those nights.

Buses came through town and stopped at the bars, then took a load back to camp on the hour. With all intention of an early turn-in, the buses were missed, and the hours kept getting pushed back. However, you could be anything but late to work. (There was a bed in the women's bathroom at work that was constantly piled with women sleeping it off. I refrained, not out of honor, but of fear of the well-worn, bald mattress.)

One of the most memorable ladies of the evening was called Bullets. She was a buxom blond and wore a skin-tight white shirt and pants, had a huge butterfly on her chest and one on her behind, and wore a belt full of bullets slung across her hips—thus her name, Bullets. Imagine one spot of curvaceous white among the throngs of brown and gray clothed people.

The women of the evening had a territory in the bars where no one else was welcome, especially new ladies in the trade. They ran a booming business and did not seem put off by scraggly beards and sometimes grubby overalls.

I suspect most boom towns have much the same pattern. It was certain that not everyone wished to be caught up in the party. Sometimes it was fun, and sometimes it felt like the world had been turned inside out—one could easily come on the feeling, *what's it all about?* There were many Friday and Saturday nights one easily remembered the next day was just another work day, and the bed was more attractive than the party.

Through all of this, September through May—the snow. Flakes would come down as big and pure as quarters. They landed on our jackets and let us inspect them for a sparkling moment. The snow was awesome in its volume and steadiness. The weather in Valdez is warm enough that there was a constant cycle of snow and melt, snow and melt. Potholes in the ice would give one a fierce knee-deep foot bath in a second of inattention. Snow levels reached roof and above. The plows with their back-up beepers ran 24 hours a day.

At the office one day was much like the next. Hiring was down as the construction became more complete. Yet, one day a woman came to apply for a staff job. It was my job to test her office skills. She was tall with a mane of dark hair and a very pretty face. She was extremely feminine, fingers and rings flashing, jewelry dangling, silk rippling—and I felt like a drudge in jeans walking next to her. All heads turned as she walked down the hall. She had on a silk jump-suit, a pretty neck scarf, a stylish purse, and high-heeled dress shoes. She was from outer space as far as we were concerned.

I could only wonder how she had gotten to the door of our building without sinking up to her ankles in mud. Her long fingernails caught in the typewriter as we tested her skill, which was poor. But she was so sweet, I passed her anyway.

I sent her off for her interview with our Texas-based manly-man, high-stepping boss. My manager Bill seemed to be choking to death in his cubicle. I'd been through this interview situation and was pulling for her. Then, the big boss made a big show of taking our head-turner to lunch, in town no less, which was cause for much speculation.

After they left, Bill, my manager, could contain himself no more. "Couldn't you see?"

"See what? She was really nice. And she came all this way to try for a job."

"That was not a woman."

I did a mental review. Being from California, I figured Bill would know. The heavily made-up face, the neck scarf, the low voice...

Given the show that macho-big-boss made of taking this striking woman to lunch, and coming back late and alone, the whole office swam underwater with laughter at the idea of him making a pass at her person. I had a good-old-boy story to tell at the dinner table that night. It took us some time to get over our joy from that event.

I befriended the camp photographer who helped me learn how to use my SLR Olympus OM1, arguably the best brand and model on the planet. It was ridiculously expensive, and anywhere else would have been put in the sport's car category. But we had all day to obsess over this fabulous camera, and to consider how much money we were not spending on housing, food, and cars. So SLR camera fever, and lusting after different brands and lenses, swept through the camp.

Generally, we sent our photos out in a special envelope for processing, and anxiously awaited the return package in the mail. Cameras and calibrator computers were the coolest camp purchases, then gold nugget watches and necklaces. People with money have to find some way to spend it.

The camp photographer let me develop some photos in her darkroom. Around camp, cameras with huge, long lenses hung around most people's necks. In the name of photos, one could almost always catch a ride to another part of the site to check it out and take artsy shots of the tank farm, the berths, or the new stack. Photos of black and brown bears rummaging in desks and trash cans became common.

Still, the first stop people made after their shift was to a huge main rec hall that had a post office, and most important, the mail boxes. That was the day of the letter. Phone calls from Alaska were not easily made, and there were lines behind a bank of pay phones available there. These calls from Alaska were expensive, limited, and four hours earlier than the east coast.

We had no computers, email, texting or twittering—letters from home or love letters were precious. Processed photos were just as popular as they popped up in in our little mailboxes. Photos were to be shared with thoughtful review to the artfulness and clarity by everyone within reach.

First call after work was a rush on the mail boxes. But the rec hall had a snack area filled with brownies, sandwiches, cookies, chips, fruit, sodas, ice cream, and such so one could divert from the mess hall if not in the mood. It also made it easy to put on extra pounds as everyone was aware. There was a make-shift movie theatre that was well attended by guys wrapped in outdoor gear that steamed in the heat of the hall. The smells were memorable. The *Texas Chainsaw Massacre* is the kind of movies I tried to miss. It was very popular. That and *The Pink Panther*.

Also, work-place entrepreneurs brought cases of jewelry back with them after their R&Rs. Rings of gold, gold nuggets, silver, turquoise, and coral were favorites. Another side sales job was to buy an Alaska map cut from the actual pipeline pipe—two-thirds of an inch thick solid steel. Highly frowned upon, therefore secretive, and a must have. Yes, I did.

In late winter cabin fever set in hard. The windows were covered with snow, it was dark all the time, and the routine was relentless. My dining buddies and I decided to rent a van on a Sunday, and go exploring. It was a great adventure, at first. We went over the stunning and notoriously dangerous, high, and narrow Thompson Pass, which was well cleared and welcomed us with uncommon bright sunlight. We diverted to Chitna, Alaska, where a bumper sticker says: where the hell is Chitna? It says that for a reason. We went to the old roadhouse there which has since burnt down.

I talked the guys into pulling over so I could take photos. I'd chosen to use black and white film, and the day was so bright that I could have dropped the camera and gotten a good photo.

The view at Gun Site Pass was classic black and white—miles of snow, part of it populated by skinny black spruce. The mountain range backed up what is now popular snow machine country. It was a lonely and forbidding spectacle stretching out without relief beside the rollercoaster road. If one tried to imagine, (and how could one not), being way out there trying to survive it looked stunningly desolate.

Then the guys got the bright idea to head for Anchorage and see how it went. We did not know how many hard hours on winter-buckled roads it would take to get there. (During the cold weather the pavement expands making frost heaves, peaks in the pavement, every 20 feet or so). It is like riding a carnival ride—especially when the driver keeps the petal to the medal. To my great dismay, the nearer we got to Anchorage, the more destination fixed my companions became. Two of the guys laid on the bench seats of the van and buckled themselves down so they could take naps and wouldn't be jarred out of their bench seats.

They slept! Impossible. It was a carnival ride. The van bounced so hard it worked the tops off a tube of lotion in my purse, and a bottle of aspirin. It was like riding a boat in a choppy ocean—for what ended up being about 20 hours total. Yes, we made it to Anchorage and ate at McDonalds. I took photos to prove our miserable claim. After McDonalds, reality hit. We were at the halfway point of our trip. We knew exactly how far we had to go back. There was no calling in sick or out of town, period. And we knew the road got worse, not better.

As we bucked our way back to Glennallen, I felt beat to pieces. We were looking forward to Thompson Pass, the last leg of the trip into Valdez. At the pass, we were suddenly in white-out conditions. (That means one can't see the nose or tail of their own vehicle because of the dense snow falling out of the sky.) It was snowing so hard we kept to the road by opening the passenger side windows, and reaching out to gauge our position on the road by using the plowed walls of snow as a boundary. Seeing ahead was impossible. Stopping was out of the question. If one dared to stop a vehicle it would immediately become overwhelmed with snow and stuck—and then would probably be hit by another vehicle.

Thompson Pass is a truckers' highway, busy with serious truckers providing supplies to the Valdez site, and time was money. As we scanned wide-eyed to try and see through a white wall, to make sure one of the trucks didn't run into us, or us them, our eyeballs bugged. We came upon a car stuck in the middle of the road and nearly hit it. The guys jumped out of our rolling van, went and pushed the car, and jumped back into the rolling van so that we didn't get stuck too.

The cords in our necks were strung tight. It was such a relief to finally come upon a big wheeler, we stayed pasted to its red tail lights. If he was going over a cliff, we were too. This at 15 MPH, which makes the drive interminable. I've never been so exhausted in my life as when we arrived back at the Valdez Airport.

In the fun leg of our trip I had cut pussy willows to put in a vase in my room—a sign of spring. Getting back on the bus to go camp with my pussy willows brought a lot of off-color attention. I wanted to smack those guys with my fuzzy willows, but settled into the truth that our get-away had been doomed to the very end, and I may as well endure another forty minutes. It was very late, and none of we travelers wanted to lose our jobs. Breakfast was blurry as a hangover. It was a long day.

Not content to try the Valdez to Anchorage trip once, I went with a girlfriend after shift Saturday, to turn around and come back Sunday. It was summer. It wouldn't be snowing. As before, the pass was a feast for the eyes, but it was also under heavy construction. There were no shoulders to the road, no paint to indicate lanes. The light was on a summer high. The forests were an overwhelming velvet green, and waterfalls sparkled along the way. One feels very small and alone on this highway. It can be one of the most unfriendly, windy roads in Alaska. One is sure to feel his or her smallness on this drive.

After what seemed like five minutes in Anchorage, sleeping on a fold-out bed while children screamed in the background, we had to head back to Valdez. It wasn't as fun as it sounded. On the return trip, that same awaited last leg of the previous round trip to Anchorage, the pass, managed to be absolutely socked in. White-out pea soup fog was just as blinding as the white-out snow. Only, there was no berm for guidance. No lines painted on the road. No road shoulder to pull over and get out of the way. I was driving blind, hoping my friend could see it better than I did. My shoulders were frozen into wings above the steering wheel. The engine kept threatening to overheat, and the brakes smelled hot. Finally, my friend and I decided that she would have to walk in front of the car to make sure we were on the road because it's a long way down steep mountains from that road.

Then we heard echoes of a big truck coming behind us. The sound came waving through the fog. Our eyeballs were stressed and we had no idea where we were on this long pass—or even on the roadway. My friend got out of the car and pointed me to the side of the road, as close as we dared to get. The only thing I could think to do was honk our horn and flip our lights, and wait for the trucker. Our light disappeared but the horn echoed through the pass.

## Trans-Alaska Pipeliner

The truck finally eased around us, and I pasted myself to his bumper and tail lights. Where he was going, that's where we were going, at 15 mph—for hours—possibly over a cliff. But the engine cooled and the brakes cooled and my friend and I agreed to follow the trucker's bumper tight to town, or to hell.

There is a bumper sticker with *skull and crossbones*, with Thompson Pass printed in the middle. I have it. We had white-out fog all the way to Valdez and it took us many hours to get there. I could barely lift my arms the next day.

With a young person's energy, one could take the bus to town after shift and shop. There was a shoe store, a grocery store, jewelry and native arts shops, restaurants, and my favorite, the drug store. It resembled the old general store—there was a little bit of everything you could imagine: prescriptions and over the counter medications, food, snacks, bed sheets, blankets, boots, flannel shirts and jeans, socks, powders and perfume, all sizes of gear bags, gloves, appliances, office supplies, fishing gear, rugs, candy, camera film, jewelry, native arts, foods, popcorn poppers, toasters, coffee pots, sundries and grooming items, cassette tapes, decorative items, magazines and books—that just scratched the surface—not cheap, but available. One could feather her nest well with a visit here, and a package from home.

Speaking to the odds, obviously, the women had plenty of admirers. That may sound like an enviable situation, but it is daunting. Men fall for a woman and she might not even know who they are. Friends would get romantic feelings that were as intense as the crazy schedule. Shortly after coming to the camp I met a man and we dated most of the time I was there. In a way, I dated the dinner table of guy-friends that I sat with for most every meal. My *'boyfriend'* was handsome, but he was a tight wad, and very self-important. I thought I was in love, but I wonder if I was seeing him more as a self-defense response: *I have a boyfriend.* It made me a safer female and friend.

This pipeline relationship wasn't done well in light of sorting out why my marriage relationship didn't work, and what I'd done wrong. Very few pipeline romances stuck. It was like leaving a space station and coming back to earth. One place was nothing like the other. We were all a little construction-site-shocked.

Most of the time the men on the site were remarkably polite and solicitous. However, sometimes in the mess hall or the rec hall we would hear a lonely male worker holler at a passing woman: *just wait till you get back to the real world and get ugly again*! That never made anyone feel better.

As construction neared completion, the pink RIF (reduction in force) slips flew. The mess hall closed in stages. The rush to get to the mail boxes became a trickle. Finally, it was my turn. I went from a hot-dog worker with a van, every appliance one could need, and a room to myself, to unemployed. The excitement and rush was turned off like a burner on the gas stove.

The folk back home now thought I was crazy. I was. We didn't speak the same language. They couldn't provide the camp camaraderie and sense of mission. The hours of meals and planning for future jobs in the mess hall—these were a thing of the past. It's not possible to live like that and then come back to the real world without many a bump—and the feeling, *I'm no longer helping to build something the world is paying attention to. The oil is in, and the world rolls on its same old way. I no longer have a cool job, or any job. Where's the next construction site?*

Due to the kindness of others, I'd visited almost every facility on the site, and dealt with almost every kind of workplace politics, romance, and even the unlikely purse theft by a coworker. The thief had seriously bitten one woman who crossed her. I decided to let it go.

I took the last commuter bus from Valdez to Anchorage, as the construction folk turned the terminal over to the production folk. The turning birch trees gave up their yellow leaves. It was deep fall, and as I look back, I'm left with the impression of a highway paved with gold. And a great void. I had been part of something monumental. I hadn't seen a kid or a pet or a current movie or a TV show in more than a year. No celebrations or holidays. I swore like all the folk on the site, which is not appropriate anywhere else. Bloomed out fireweed painted the fields and mountains pink in fall. Who would have thought an adventure that started with so many what-ifs and worries would deliver one of the great adventures of my lifetime? But, this pipeline stint delivered much more than that. It delivered a certain kind of fearlessness. If I could handle the hours and conditions of work on the pipeline, the politics, and the loss of dear friends who knew me better than my family, I could handle anything.

There were no sick days in a construction camp. Friends were like gold. Letters were a life line. The pace and production of a world class facility was addictive. I'd learned when to wear a hard hat, and never to wear a powder-blue pantsuit to a construction site. (And I learned not to drive to Anchorage from Valdez for a hamburger.)

The Valdez Pipeline Terminal is a work-horse facility now with its tank farms and ocean-going-tankers docking, filling, and steaming away.

Still, every time I see the Trans-Alaska Pipeline, from the air or from the ground, I am awed. I think of the men and women who lived in the camps and built this engineering wonder, and I feel like I was privileged to experience a part of history in the making—a part in provisioning the thirsty USA with Alaska-USA oil.

Yes, I wanted go back.

PS: Most of us looked forward to the next Alaska gas pipeline construction which was left hanging out there with a "soon" sign. We kept in touch with our employers and finally had to realize the fact that due to politics, another pipeline wouldn't be built, and we would never have that experience again. It took me two years to get back to, for me, normal—and to get back to Alaska. Nothing could compare to it. Nothing else would do.

# 2.

# The Helicopter and the Glacier

There are margins in the world, flying in a helicopter tests those margins. It is said that helicopters do not fly-they beat the air into submission. Alaska is a bit of a fantasy land. It takes twenty minutes to get to *impossible*.

My job was to contract helicopters and planes for the Alaska Geological Field Surveys for my company. The contractors were very kind to share their equipment with their customers. My contractor had gotten a new A-Star helicopter, and offered me a test ride.

I can get embarrassingly air sick given the right conditions. However, the opportunity to buzz over the Chugach Mountains like an eagle in flight was not to be missed.

I was able to bring two others with me, and fortunately, upper management was out of town. The pilot told us to bring our fishing poles, and I didn't have to look far for companions for this ride.

I was strapped in this beautiful, new, shiny helicopter—headphones on, looking confident—but I fingered the plastic bag tucked in my pocket. The helicopter lifted so gently that we hardly felt the lift, hovering like a humming bird at 4, 8, 12 feet, then slowly upward making our way to the Chugach foothills, skirting them until we could clearly view the magnificent Chugach Range in its sunshine glory. Denali was out in her shining best.

Because the wind was low we did not make that fwap, fwap, fwap, one sometimes hears from helicopters. Just a smooth, graceful line to the Chugach Mountains and beyond.

We rolled over the top of the mountains to the north-east and in seconds we blew from city to intimidating wilderness. There was grandeur around us of dark spruce, birch, and cottonwood reaching up the mountains like picks from a brush, dropping off at the tree line into blueberries and assorted brush. Hovering at the top of our elevation, stark white peaks of shale and snow and blue ice folded and spiked. It seemed we could see every rock, and there were no footprints in that snow.

The Chugach Mountains with their dense snow cradled these glaciers that are surprisingly close to civilization, and surprisingly untrammeled. These mountains are covered with shale and rotten ice, and so steep that climbing is high risk, which may be why climbing Denali is more popular.

Then the pilot dropped down beside a deeply crackled, sheer wall of blue glacier—a gigantic, jagged passage between two walls. Like a polished gemstone, patterns of cracks reached deep into the blue. It was inconceivable. Where did this magic kingdom come from? How few people know that this massive gemstone lies just over their mountains?

Like God's parting the waters, two walls lay before us with a striking channel between. One could look into the ancient blue wall of ice and without much imagination picture ice fossils of sticks leaves, and suspicious things. No one could say how old that ice was. The glacial blue was as deep as a meditation as we glided through a V shaped channel, the crack in the glacier. The pilot expertly negotiated his course. I dreaded the end that must come soon. One could feel the prehistoric freeze reaching to these

# The Helicopter and the Glacier

current times. There was a thread of history braided through the ice. It was anciently cold. We were on a magic carpet.

I wanted to go on forever, but the channel, as it must, came to an end. How could anything be greater than that? We climbed over another mountain top to skim down into the low land where we wandered above birch, willow, cottonwood, and spruce trees. The sun was bright, and we saw dozens of pot-hole lakes, strands of water, and a rich carpet of moss.

There were occasional moose resting or tip-toeing in the grass, water, and moss. In a helicopter it feels as if one could reach out and touch the trees and the land. (There is a syndrome that causes some people to feel as if they can get out of the helicopter and walk.)

With a dip and a turn we were over a crazy beautiful islanded lake, and the helicopter touched down. We got out our fishing poles, and stood on the fallen logs and caught grayling. I can still picture the four of us standing, casting into the water, reeling in the fish—in another world—made all the more unreal by the fact that this was during *work* hours! People were back at the office laboring away. Here, there were no other fishers to tangle lines, there was no trash on the bank. There were no bears or moose at the lake, only eagles and water-birds. Through bottle green waters one could see the lake's bottom. The needle-nosed pike and fingerlings cruised by and through water grasses. I loved my job.

Late in the day we reluctantly returned to Anchorage. The sky was still the evening-bright of summer. The orange hangar was silhouetted by the mountains. None of us were in a hurry to get back to real life. Climbing from the helicopter felt as if one had passed through another dimension. Walking to, and getting into a common old car, was a hard reminder of being back to the bounds of earth. There seemed to be more gravity now.

After a day like this, one almost wonders if it really happened at all.

<u>Rule of Helicopters</u>

## An Alaskan Woman Writes Again

Never ignore the weather
Never be in a hurry
Always go if you have the chance

3.

# The Sled Dogs and the Momma Bear

My husband and I have had three rescue sled dogs over the years.* Because rescue dogs lived harder lives, they sometimes don't live as long as other dogs.

> *Note: Most mushers and dog lots are run with nurturing, responsibility, and care. You never see a race photo where the dog doesn't look at its owner with devotion and trust. The loving human-canine relationships, and the desire to run, are obvious to anyone who has ever seen these dogs and their drivers. The dogs are considered super-athletes. Having a dog lot is a 24-hour-a-day, seven-days-a-week job. Irresponsible and careless dog owners are held in low regard, and have their teams taken from them.*

Our three rescue girls came to us at various ages—each with some signs of wear and frostbite that made them precious to us.

These dogs are so sweet and appreciative that I cannot imagine adopting anything but a rescue sled dog. They have been raised outside, on a chain, with their own small wood dog house or igloo. (They are chained to prevent fighting because there are always a few alphas.) They love to pull and to run, and they jump high in the air and howl when their musher brings out their food or their sled.

Sled dogs, for the most part, don't look like the picturesque broad-chested malamute with long, dense fur. They have short fur, long legs, and are made of a secret recipe of shepherd, lab, Doberman, husky, and who knows what other breed—somehow, they all have similar faces and physiques. And it looks like they all wear Cleopatra eye-make-up. Still, there are people who run poodles and malamutes.

Our experience is with rescue dogs. These sled dogs live year around outside. Adopted sled dogs are anywhere from a year or two old, to seniors, so they've gone through the puppy phase. They don't tend to develop habits like jumping up on people or going potty indoors. They tend to confine their chewing to their bones and their toys. They don't tend to jump on the counters or get in the trash. They are very smart and pick up on hand signals, and moods quickly. They tend to be submissive and very lovey, and shake their collar to signal *it's time to go out*, or say, *I'm ready for a dog biscuit*. Dogs are social animals. They do need plenty of companionship (as do all dogs) and don't make good *gone-for-12-hours-day* dogs.

Our current dog, Rose, had one of her feet run over when she was a pup, so her foot is like a pancake, flat, and she stands with her leg turned out as if to say, *I'm waiting*. She is what a friend calls a *love sponge*. She lets the grandkids lay on her with great patience, and blends in when the gang is all present.

Our three dogs did not roam far from us when off the leash. We didn't have to worry about them running off. They knew they'd been adopted, and found a good home.

They all loved snow-baths and looked ridiculous as they lay on their backs and scoot and wiggle, up-side-down, on the snow-covered driveway, from the top to the bottom (a long way). They all tend to sleep with their body on their dog bed, and their heads on the floor. I don't know why. I just know that their love is sweet and pure, and they are easier to be with than many people.

Each of our dogs has a collection of silly ways, but it was Rose, who laid by me on the deck on this warm, clear afternoon in early fall.

We Alaskans count the hours when it is comfortable enough to sit outside dressed in a tee shirt and capris, with a slight breeze to keep away the mosquitoes. I had my feet up, some iced tea, and a couple of favored magazines. Rose, lay beside me dozing, her black fur soaking in the sun.

We'd been pleased to see that Rose doesn't become aggressive with moose and calves, and bears and cubs. On a winter walk she stepped up to one moose who was laying down in the snow— the moose didn't bother to get up. They touched noses, looked each other over, and as good as said: hi. They both went back to their business.

This day, all was good on the sunny deck. Then, Rose was gone. I heard ferocious barking and growling. I jumped up and turned to look down the hill. About eight yards away, Rose was chest to chest with a healthy sized sable black bear. They were both growling and barking, standing on their back legs, their mouths wide open in attack, their back fur standing on end. Momma Bear's puff-ball twin cubs went up the birch trees so fast they could have beat out a cat. They clung up there in the top of the trees like little bear clip toys. All of this hit my eyes and mind in a flash. Then I start yelling my head off.

Everyone knows the odds are in the bear's favor, especially when she has cubs.

We are smack in the middle of bear and moose country. In the summer my husband and I often tease, with a basis in reality, and say: *cover me, I'm going to change the sprinklers.*

I was up hill from the two fighters, so I was waving my arms in order to look big, (a recommended but generally futile behavior in the face of an angry bear), and making a lot of noise. I happened to have black on which would have made me look bigger from down below, and I had magazines flapping in each hand. It was reflex to jump up, yell, and wave my arms. I knew that Rose would be torn up. Nothing grapples with a big, black bear and comes out whole.

I was making so much noise, they both paused and looked at me. I called Rose and she came running for me. My husband came running for me. So did the bear. I was jumping up and down throwing such a fit, the momma bear stopped about 15 feet out, paused, and gave a look that said: *she's just too much trouble*.

Momma turned and went in a huff back down the hill and signaled her cubs to come down. They came down the trees as fast as they had gone up. Momma-bear looked back with an insulted air, we had rudely interrupted her afternoon stroll. She and her two black-fur-ball kids disappeared into the trees.

Rose jumped on the deck, thrilled with herself. We both inspected her carefully, looking for blood, punctures, and tears. After all, there had been all that growling and snapping, barking, and chest to chest fighting—but there was not a visible wound on Rose that we could find. She has a thick coat even in the summer. It seemed impossible that no hunks were missing. It felt like God was there providing a simple mercy. (We are devastated when something happens to our dogs. Rose was only about five years old.)

Rose was very stiff the next day, and she shed about half of her fur in the next two days. A self-defense, trauma response I suppose—and a hairy mess. Rose was quite proud to have saved me from the bear. Dick praised Rose. I scolded her for jumping in the middle of a bear and her cubs. She didn't pay any attention to me.

We are over-the-top about our dogs. Rescue sled dogs tend to be very sweet and polite. Except when they perceive wild animals as a threat. Unfortunately, it is common for the bear to follow its intruder back to the owner. It could have gone bad, as it has done many times on our hill. Both of us were very fortunate.

As my granddaughter and I were driving down the hill a few days after the momma bear incident, this same mom-bear stepped out of the brush beside the road. I stopped, and she stood beside the car looking in. She had no fear. Her look was: *yeah, I let you off easy*. For once we had a camera ready and took her picture. This was a big, healthy, sable black bear. Her cubs were in the brush. She checked us out, and melted away as if she'd never been.

The moral of the story is: any confrontation with a bear that comes out without blood is a good one.

*Our wonderful adoption agency is: **Friends of Pets** (907) 333-9534

P.O. Box 240981, Anchorage, Alaska 99524-0981, www.friendsofpets.org

4.

# For the Love of TV in Winter

It's January in Anchorage, and I'm standing on the roof of my three story house. The distant city lights are a washed out blur as snow keeps sifting down. White rain. Because we do get snowed in, and because our locations are not exactly population centers, many Alaskans have TV dishes. The trouble with dishes is that they fill up with snow and the TV screen goes relentlessly black.

One can gaze at a black screen, or grab a broom and climb out a small window on to a steep roof, and step into waist-deep snow. I mean, really, how hard can it be to traverse a little mountain of snow, with a broom, and boots, and in pajamas?

I was snowed in and going nowhere. Alaskans are perverse. Don't tell us we can't go get groceries, or go to a movie in the middle of a blizzard or hurricane force winds. It becomes an obsession. I needed the TV for company, and a reading companion, and because it wasn't there.

My husband is usually the dish sweeper, thunking across the roof, stomping around, wary of the potential three story fall—all for the love of sports. Most shows are not worth risking a fingernail, but we will not have our TV taken away from us. We will gallantly defy the snow with a possibility of breaking our necks for a pack of mind-numbingly repetitive commercials.

I didn't realize how far it was from the window to the dish. I didn't realize I had to move from one roof line to another. I didn't remember that snow on the roof is much more compacted by heat from the house. It was like walking through thigh-high mashed potatoes. Cold ones.

The broom took turns as a pitiful shovel and a walking stick as I inched toward the dish. I had put on a coat, but with the exertion I was adding to the humidity and drips were falling from my nose. Finally, the dish came in view, and it seemed to be in an awfully edgy place. I anchored myself and used my broom like a four foot long paintbrush, dabbling the snow from the dish. Finally, I had done all I could. With mountain climbing exertion, I was warm, the snow stuck to every part of me, even my eyelashes, making every slogging step an event. I am fascinated by the mental set of those who must climb Denali. I have never had any desire to climb Denali myself. This experience did not change my mind.

I came back in the window with no grace what so ever, dumping myself and snow on the floor, and making it as far as the bathroom before it became imperative to get this combination of flannel and snow off my back.

I don't have a punchline where the TV doesn't work after I come back in. At least I don't for 24 hours. At least there was a trail to follow on my second trip. TV was awful.

5.

# North to Alaska

I was in the south of Alaska, hundreds of miles from the smallest town, and I wasn't sure that I was actually on the road—any road. I was on my own, and hadn't seen anyone for hours. Not even construction equipment. How did I get here?

After having worked on the Trans-Alaska Pipeline, we employees thought that we would be called back shortly to work on the Alaska *gas line*. Those from Alaska know that the gas line is still in contention today—35 years later. So much for a three year plan.

I had traveled to the USA and Mexico for a few months, got restless, and moved from Idaho to Jacksonville, Florida. A girlfriend from pipeline days lived there.—Talk about culture shock. If the pipeline was its own planet, then the south and Florida was its own country. The north and the deep south have entirely different personalities, language, climate, buggy-ness, and geology. I loved the ocean off Florida, the eateries were second to none, and I loved the farmers' markets, and oranges, but I did not love snakes or alligators or shoe-sized insects. In Florida, if your family doesn't have at least three generations back, you're new.

Every day, on my way to work in Florida, I drove past a building with a white gravel roof, and every time I glanced to that roof, for a second I thought it was the mountains. (Florida is the flattest state in the USA.) And every day I was disappointed. Finally, I decided that my true love was Alaska, and set out to drive from Jacksonville, Florida, to Anchorage, Alaska –about as far as it is possible to travel and stay on the ground in the USA and Canada.

I left a boyfriend. He wasn't a prize, but I thought him precious. We had broken up over him wrecking my car, again, among other expensive things. My Dad had made me promise not to fall for a southern man, but I didn't listen. I should have. It didn't make the hurt any less.

I held over in Houston with family, and then stopped in Coeur d'Alene, Idaho (back home) on my way back to Anchorage. I had a passenger for the Houston to Coeur d'Alene portion of the drive. My mom. We did survive. That drive was a 'bucket list' drive through the flat land of the south and the highways over water, to the city of Houston which has great restaurants, up through the southwest and Carlsbad (and the awesome caverns), to the Grand Canyon, and on up through Zion National Park, and the Rocky Mountains in the spring of the year. I was supposed to have a two week hold-over before leaving for Anchorage on the Alaska Marine Highway ferry system.

While in Idaho, one day at lunchtime, as we left the mall, my sister and I stepped outside to see the sky was filled with dark depths of grainy black clouds. My sister and I seriously thought we might be seeing the end of the world. It was May, 1980, and Mt. Saint Helens had blown her lid. Communications were not as fast then. No texts or smart phones. While Mt. St. Helens had been threatening to erupt, we ignored the news coverage and had no concept of how far she would reach, and how much unparalleled damage and loss of life Mt. Saint Helens would cause. It became a *before and after* line in people's lives.

Auto travel essentially shut down for weeks while piles of ugly gray ash blew through the air and heaped beside the roads. It had a texture similar to talcum powder. Try sweeping that.

The ash was death on engines. Air filters for one's vehicle became precious, then unattainable, and people reverted to pantyhose as air filters. People with breathing difficulties were warned to stay inside. The few people who were out wore face masks. My trip to Alaska on the Alaska Marine Highway System was stalled in a powdery, dusty gray land. My travel money was disappearing at an alarming rate. I had to get to Alaska and find a job.

Volcanic ash is depressing. It is fine, glass-like dust that sifts into every crevasse and crack and door and window. It scratches everything. Green lawns look black. Every piece of furniture inside and out was covered with dust. The only thing worse is wet volcanic ash. Mud poured off the roof when it rained. Dark puddles and black rain did nothing to make people hopeful. Every home, restaurant, and store had black foot tracks in and out. And paper towels and mops couldn't cope with the volume or texture.

My newish little red car was an ash ball, and the dust scratched all the surfaces. Little did I know that this smite of ash was nothing compared to driving trials to come on my drive in Alaska.

When the highway between states finally re-opened, I drove from Idaho, all the way across a gray Washington state on a highway (a five hour drive I'd taken many dozens of times) that generally had high traffic. At this time that highway was nearly empty, and eerie. The mountains and the farm lands were blanketed with gray dust. But, I had an appointment with the Alaska Ferry System departing Alaska Way, Washington, on my way to Haines.

I'd had mom ride with me during part of the eventful trip across the L-48, but I was again on my own.

This was a bit of an Alaska Pipeline replay. I didn't have a clue what I was getting into on the first trip—nothing—and my only direction for this destination was Anchorage, Alaska. There's only one road from Haines to Anchorage, right? How hard could that be? I didn't have a job, but I was pretty sure I'd have a place to sleep. I didn't know anything about the town except some pipeline friends lived there. I hope I would prepare better now than then. At the time, I progressed only by falling forward rather than back.

With my hatch-back car densely packed up through the passenger seat, my Mom gave me a stuffed eagle to ride shotgun on the arm rest. I named him Elliot, and Elliot was going to get an unbelievable ride.

I was afraid I'd be late to the ferry and didn't refill my gas tank before driving on board the Ferry. It's hard to find a gas station in down town Seattle. This was a mistake. But, I would be getting off the ferry in Haines, which would surely have gas stations. Surely.

As I drove my car on board the ferry, my heart was filled with the idea that I would have four days on the ferry, I would ride through Canada and back to Alaska, and I couldn't be happier. There was no point in worrying about anything in that time suspended on water. So for once in my life, I took advantage of the mental and physical break.

While at dock I walked the decks and checked out the ship. I had planned to sleep on the outdoor sleeping deck. That deck was squirming full with families and singles, and all the space under an overhang had been claimed so that there was no room on the camping pad. I decided to take my chances and went to pair up for a berth in a room. It boiled down to me and three seniors sharing a four birth room. It was that or the hard deck. So I joined them and split the cost. As it turned out, they were the best traveling companions, thoughtful, kind, and interesting. I was afraid I'd wake them coming and going—no such worry. Each bunk is very private. One equalizer is the constant thrum of the engines which cover all superficial noise. The other is that they were taking part in every event offered and preferred playing cards to sleep.

People on the ferry were very friendly, but I still felt like a standalone. The second day I pushed my way (something I learned, not something I did easily) into a newly formed group of three great companions. The young woman had gone from working in Prudhoe Bay and decided to give commercial fishing a try. I thought her fiancé would be happy to have her on board his boat. One fellow was a social worker from New Mexico. This was his Alaska adventure. The other fellow was taking a kayak trip down some mostly uncharted rivers to write and photograph an article for National Geographic.

We formed a tight group and met up for meals, talk, programs, and to share ports of call. It would be very hard to peel off from this group when we got to Haines, where everyone would go their own way. That travel-friend syndrome follows where traveling with strangers leads to people sharing their thoughts, wishes, and worries more honestly than one might with a good friend. The congenial pleasure became impossible to extend after leaving the ferry. We were all heading to different life destinations. Here, I would start alone on what would turn out to be the most challenging drive of my life. When the time came, I wanted to turn around and get back on the ferry.

Our group would spend a lot of time on the decks with eye glasses and cameras trying to hold on to the majesty we quietly passed. Trying to describe this tangled craggy wilderness, trees, slivers of sand, and swarms of islands with *words* is like trying to capture it with a *photo*. Justice cannot be done. Giving my eyes the gift and lift of unpopulated, densely forested, and steep, spiky, buckling mountains, scents of pine and spruce and coastal waters, was like a tonic. Birds keened and swept by the ferry, and an occasional bear or elk would be at the water's edge in the Alexander Archipelago. The textured shades of green were awe inspiring.

We passed the crazy-wild west Canadian coast, Queen Charlotte Sound, Prince Rupert, and the St. Elias Range while in the Gulf of Alaska. Formidable rocky cliffs held no sign of cabins. Those mountains are very self-confident, they don't care what we think. Fearsomely remote, we passed encapsulated in the safety of an Alaska Highway Ferry.

Clouds billowed and striated across the sky. I felt like I could breathe again for the first time in a very long time. The air was cool and a pleasure to my body. I was in the scene like "Titanic" (the good part) where they stand with their arms out, holding the wind, at the bow of the ship. I had packed my down jacket for the trip and felt protected to be folded in its feathery hold once again. It's amazing how long one can stand at the rail of a ferry heading north.

We stopped in Ketchikan, Wrangell, Petersburg, Juneau—last stop for me, Haines. These towns seem to hang on the edge of the mountains over a narrow shelf of shoreline. A common and charming sight revealed that most of the towns had extensive docks, boardwalks, and houseboats, all of which invite a person to walk every turn.

It is not hard to imagine what it was like there 100 years ago. It's not hard to imagine wanting to live there. This is the land of the totem. Wrangle had the most ancient totem poles, Ketchikan has the largest collection of totem poles, and is the first port of call for north-bound ships.

South Alaska art is known for its striking graphic artistry, texture, and use of colors that you want to touch, or own. At each stop I asked myself, could I live here? I thought that I could. Yet, one has to be able to deal with rain, downpours, mist, sleet, and more rain year around.

The days on the ferry are among the most peaceful in my life. We had mostly sunshine, and we had the rare pleasure of having to do nothing, and no time schedule to follow we stopped in Juneau it was the middle of the night. Juneau is the capital city and from the ferry dock looks uncommonly modern with many tall business buildings. My photographer friend patiently helped me take pictures of Juneau at night, testing apertures, savoring the time and place and color and smell. One of those pictures later won a photo contest.

# North to Alaska

We arrived in Haines at 5:30am, which was the place of departure for many people on the ferry. It broke my heart to say goodbye to the great people I had come to know. Travelers are given to sharing and creating new treasured memories. However, always at the back of my mind, was the need for fuel for my car. I continue to reason that Haines is a pretty good size town, and it has to have a gas station. Didn't it? Nobody I talked to was sure. Then what?

The pamphlet said Haines was established to police northern gold camps. It is also a pivotal point in which to join the Alcan. Fishing and mining remained important to the area. Haines made me wait until 8:30am to get my fuel! Three hours!!! I finally found gas pumps—the kind that you hand-pump to get the fuel up into a clear bowl at the top of the fuel pump, then gravity drops it into the gas tank. Most everyone had raced past me, out of town long before I was able to hit the road. I was counting on other highway company and had none. About 30 miles out of Haines was the Canadian Border and the end of paved roads. It occurs to me now that I had an insufficient map, and no plan except to drive north. (Never do these roads without the latest Milepost.)

At the border there was no line waiting to get through, all had passed hours earlier. I showed my drivers' license to the agent, told him where I was going, Anchorage, and proved I had $500—enough to get through Canada and back to Anchorage. (People streaming up to try for work on the pipeline on a song and a prayer, and in a ratty car, had left Canadians holding the *homeless bag*. So there was a $500 requirement at the border.)

The RCMP teased me about my undeclared rider, Elliot. At this point I was getting a little panicked by the lack of company, and my lack of preparation for this part of the trip. I got tears in my eyes, and he quickly waved me through before I had a breakdown.

My mother did plan as far as food, packed a cooler where I was able to keep ice from the ferry. I had grapes and cheese and crackers, oatmeal cookies, and some drinks in a cooler. Who knew where there would be a place to eat? I did not know the next 420 miles were under extreme construction, that I should have taken another route, and there were times when I was not sure I was on a road at all. I did not know why the plow drivers were so aggressive, forcing me off the road and never looking back. Because, I shouldn't have been on the road at all.

At one point the mud was so deep that I had to keep the gas petal to the floor in order to not get stuck. The idea of being stuck alone in no man's land kept me driving like a pro mud wrestler. I don't remember much about scenery. At times I questioned if I had taken the wrong road to nowhere. There were no vehicles. I felt lost, but kept to a trail that looked most likely. My shoulders cramped with the tension of driving and trying to see the road. It all looked like one big mud pit.

Out of Haines I had to decide between Highway 7 or 2. I decided to go on Highway 7 as it looked like the most efficient (?) choice. Two would have lead me essentially away from Alaska to Whitehorse, Yukon Territory, which would have been one heck of a detour, essentially making the trip twice the length it would be on Highway 2. It would have been better advised. But I was in a hurry. My money was going quickly and I had to get a job. Now, I wonder why I didn't take the road better traveled and enjoy my last days of unemployment.

The road climbed and wended and coursed through changing topography. Much of the route was said to be made on the Indians pathways. I came to a point where I had to make another decision: Highway 1 or Highway 1. I went left on Highway 1 west, which under normal circumstances would have been the best route. However, I didn't know it was under full bore, scrape to the ground construction. The fact soon became obvious, but I thought it was a temporary snag. Alaska and Canada are famous for runs of construction dotting the highway that go for five miles, or 12 miles, so I wasn't alarmed at first.

Like knobs on a chain I would drive Highway 1 from Haines, to Haines Junction—past Kluane Lake and on to Burwash Landing,

Kluane, Beaver Creek, and Port Allen. These are places you could miss if you glanced at your speedometer.

Just when I thought the road couldn't get worse, three huge plows with huge blades drove straight for me taking the entire road! There was a three foot high dirt berm in the middle of this very narrow road. It was like playing *chicken* with monster plows. They clearly were not going to move or stop for me, so I belly flopped my little car through the berm and nearly got high centered, staggered around the nearly nonexistent shoulder while the plows dozed on, then had to cross back to my "lane" with another dramatic belly flop. Sweating, I was glad to have that ordeal behind me. How much more could my rear-wheel-drive compact take? Except I had to do the dirt belly flop over and over and over. And over. Every time I thought I would get high-centered. (I would find that the road had sprung my car door and bent the frame of my car!) With no choice, I leaned forward and put the gas to the floor. It wasn't braveness, it was survival. I guess I could have gone back to the ferry and returned to my home town. It never entered my mind. I kept thinking that the worst of the road must be behind me.

My car was less than a year old, and it was not my habit to drive a dirty car. Mt. Saint Helens had strained my clean car expectations, and there was probably still ash in the crevasses. Now I was a ball of mud. I was hoping for a carwash along the highway. I'm not kidding, I actually thought there would be one. There were no car washes.

To add to the joy, rarity of pit stops, and bouncing around the rough roads that were in place, and the stress—I got a bladder infection. There were no quick-stops along this road. This added another dimension to my trip. Fortunately, I had cranberry juice and meds with me. Still.

Along the way were a few roadhouses where there might be a car or two sitting outside. I wanted to push on through but I needed a bathroom, gas (ditch and mud diving takes a lot of gas) and a real meal. And I needed to clean off my windows. As a single woman on the road, I stuck out like a beacon. Maybe it was because I was the only uninformed person on the road. At the café I got so much questioning attention that the meal was kind-of miserable, and I was grateful to be back in the car with Elliot. Yet, no one said: are you crazy driving this way?

My red car was no longer red, it was entirely packed and splattered with brown mud and muck which was hanging off the sides. More terrible, rough road negotiation challenged me to the Alaska-Canada border. The US roadway wasn't under so much construction, but it needed to be. That highway was broken every 15 to 20 feet with frost heaves (like small teepees) crossing the whole road. One sort of flew from road bump to road bump. This highway curled like a snake, there was no road shoulder, just cliffs and fields and rocks, and plenty of potholes. The scenery, poorly seen through smeary windows, was not a consideration. At least there were some other vehicles around on this part of the highway, and much less mud. My goal was to make it, no matter how long it took, to Tok where I would rest. And it took a long time. And, I didn't know how to rest once I got there.

Tok, Alaska, an Alcan hub, was a more than welcome site. It was a real little town with paved streets. My shoulders had almost knitted themselves together by the time I drove into Tok. It was painful to put my arms down which makes for odd posture.

There, I was back in the land of $85 single modest room with gold carpet and gold vinyl curtains, and the $7 hamburger—in 1980 that was a lot. That $500 was going fast at that rate. But I was deeply grateful for the shower and bed.

When I came out to get into my car the next day, I was stopped in my tracks. People in the parking lot were standing around looking at my car. It had rained hard over the night, and there was a perfectly peaked 12" berm of mud all around the whole car. I had to go borrow a shovel in order to get in the car. The people in the parking lot were all hoping I hadn't come from the Haines highway, and I got some pleasure in describing what they had to look forward to if they went the same way. The alternative is hundreds of miles out of the way to Whitehorse, Yukon. If they were smart, they took the detour.

The drive from Tok to Anchorage was no picnic. The Wrangle Mountains make sure of that. The frost heaves continued to dissect the road, and it turns like a corkscrew. The few bridges were narrow and fragile looking, with a killer fall underneath. From Tok it is 328 miles to Anchorage. The road was something resembling normal Alaska highway traffic on a roller coaster, yet in a place where no one passed a disabled car, rather than plowing them into the ditch, I felt like I was on a super-highway. (Anyone who drives that road today would say it is always under construction, and it is a lot of work to drive mountainous and twisty roads.) I stopped at the familiar gas-hub at Glennallen. It is not a picturesque and inviting stop. So, I drove on—and swooped and bounced through the Kuskokwim Mountains and the Alaska Range on my way to Palmer, Eagle River, and finally, Anchorage.

It was 2,580 miles from Coeur d'Alene to Anchorage. I was destination-driven at this point. And my friends were waiting for me, except they weren't.

My friend that probably had a room had given me backward instructions to get to the condo where I'd be staying. The gas station attendants didn't recognize the area I was looking for, and there were no cell phones, and few pay phones. Of course, in all the papers, I couldn't find phone numbers I needed, and when I did call, no one answered. Exhausted, I was hitting the *flip-out* point.

Getting another motel room for $125 a night was not in my financial picture. After some hours, trying to drive a backward map, and phone booth, I arrived at a friend's house in Anchorage, worn to a frazzle. There was no bed, just a nice hard floor, and a condo neighbor who played rock and roll all night.

However, soon I had a bed, and found my friends, and started to negotiate Alaska's biggest city.

Still, there is a high after making it over the southern Everglades, to Houston, around the Grand Canyon, down in Carlsbad Caverns, through Zion National Park, Coeur d'Alene, Seattle, Haines, and Tok, and so many other fascinating places. It had been my job, and my body wanted to get back in the car and keep going.

With my friends' help, I had a bedroom and a bathroom. The first month's rent, three times what I was used to paying, pretty-much flattened my savings. My first purchase was a piece of black fabric. The sun never went down. I put it over the window but was surprised how little it helped. Many people turn to thick vinyl or tin foil to line their bedroom windows in the northern summer. Sleep deprived and hecticly goal oriented to get there, I was a little weird. Okay, a lot weird. A driver without a road.

Within a week, through the recommendation of my roommate, I had an oil company job. I was back in Alaska and yet feeling disconnected. Everything was two or three times more expensive than what I was used to. I didn't know anything about the town. My ex-boyfriend kept calling. I was the new kid in town and hadn't yet established a life, or even a good idea where anything was. I was trying not to be needy with the friends I did have.

The oil industry is one of the more convoluted businesses out there, nothing like construction, and my new employer were speaking another language at work. They would ask me to get the OCS file, or the ANWR file, or the AOGA file—or EOA and WOA stats and reports, and NSB statements, and on and on. My clothes were Florida, a jarring departure from Alaska.

My female manager wanted me to know what it took others two or three years to learn and showed no mercy. But, after a while I made a list of oil company acronyms, found all the departments I needed to work with, met new friends, and got the lay of the land.

The women's movement was in full swing, and I swung with it, working my butt off. The style was poofy hair, long skirts, suits, and shoulder pads. We women *were* to be taken seriously, *were* there to make our mark in the women's movement—but that *was* in our minds, not for the most part an oil company tradition.

A number of us would meet on Friday for a cocktail after work. The restaurant and bar of Harry's was located in a bank building. One evening, I was too sober, and fretting about my ex who had threatened to come to Alaska. They sun was still high and it was a warm day when I went to leave that building. I ran flat into double glass doors that I had thought were open. I broke my nose, and stumbled out to hang on a brick planter outside the bank as the world went dark. People stepped around me thinking I was drunk. I had blood running down my face and was too proud to go back in and ask for help. That was a low spot. I don't remember how I got home. My nose and eyes were black and blue—not a good look for a new job.

After a short time I reconnected with pipeline friends, and learned my way around. The city of Anchorage made more sense. Good companionship made life a lot more fun.

I washed my car my first day in town, and many times after. The driver door wouldn't shut properly ever again. The wheels looked slightly off and the tires had a strange wear-pattern. I never did get that car completely clean ever again.

I have thought of my AMC Spirit as a problematic car that never ran well, but it got me through six thousand miles across the entire US and Canada without breaking down, or running out of gas. That's kind of amazing. My AMC turned out to be the worst car ever on snow. On those winter mornings when it was 40 degrees below zero, the car felt as if it would crackle into pieces if I slammed the door. An elevation of inches stopped it cold on ice. But, it started. Looking back, driving a 1980 AMC across the continent was pretty impressive. I'd do it again. (Not the boyfriend part.)

## An Alaskan Woman Writes Again

This time I would take the detour and stop and smell the forget-me-nots along the way.

6.

# Duct Tape Cleavage

The Miners' and Trappers' Ball was the event of the season. People stood in line for hours, freezing their buns off, to capture a ticket to this costume event in February.

> Fur Rendezvous is Alaska's version of Mardi Gras. It's a two week event in February, answering to a very long winter and cabin fever, and heralding the Iditarod Sled Dog Race. The Miner's and Trapper's Ball was held in a huge business warehouse with concrete floors, and port-a-potties. Usually, about 2,000 people attended. Two bands, one at each end of the facility, kept people moving in a great oval promenade. This celebration came about with deep roots in winter restlessness. It was one of those events where it was the law that one must buy a Rondy Button, or the Rondy Police would take you to jail. One of those carts with bars on it. Not a normal jail, but a convincing way to sell buttons.

The Miners' and Trappers' Ball was coming near. My dear friend Jennifer had spent years yearning for cleavage. She took her costumes very seriously, and they were generally sexy.

After listening to her to complain once again about her flat chest I said: I can give you cleavage with duct tape if you can stand the pain.

This was when duct tape only came in silver, and was not yet used to make wallets and coats and monuments. The big night came. I have some sense of engineering and started under one arm, building a tourniquet that would squeeze her chest and made the best use of everything she had. It must have felt terrible to be trussed up with sticky, harsh, two inch wide tape. But she was thrilled with the results. She had cleavage.

In our costumes, we braved the north wind, below zero temperatures, knee deep snow, inconvenient and distant parking lots, and icy wind to be part of this celebration. Women in formals with bunny boots and fur coats marched into the building, handed over their precious tickets, and paid their many dollars for the drink of the evening, a Polar Bear. (Kahlua, vodka, and cream.)

People who have nothing else to think about in the cold and dark can be very creative when it comes to costumes. Competitions for beards by color were followed by competitions for miners and trappers, and current events themes. Skinny and fat Oprah came, Mr. and Mrs. President, as did Barney Clark and his heart replacement machine. There were cowboys without seats in their pants, Vampires, Leprechauns, three bears, birds, telephone poles, pimps and hookers, Dorothy and Toto, sports figures, Star Trek characters, Canadian Mounties, gamblers, cancan dancers, satellite dishes, M&Ms, cheese heads, cows, cowboys on horses—I could go on. Of course, this was a ball, so there were plenty of ball gowns but being Alaska, there were few tuxes.

The blue port-a-potties are a fact of life in Alaska, and in this case, ball gowns must submit. Jennifer also happens to be a frequent potty visitor and make-up applier. She dragged me and Cindy on opposite shifts to the port-a-potties to help manage her hoop skirt costume. No little event. There weren't any mirrors in these potties, so we were also expected to be her human and portable mirror. "Do I look alright, how do I look, do I need lipstick, is my hair okay?"

Of course Jennifer required red, red, red lipstick. She'd pull one of us to the port-a-potty, and drag that lipstick round and round her mouth, getting further and further outside her lip line. By the time she'd asked, for the 50$^{th}$ time, "how do I look?" Cindy and I had sort of turned into port-a-potty zombies. We'd just mumble, "you look fine, great, fine…"

Jennifer is tall, and wore high, high heels with her old-south; low-cut gown. She left a path where ever she cruised with her hoop skirt and cleavage—her accessories: a dramatic wide-brim hat, a sun umbrella, gloves, a fan, a purse, a shawl, feathers, and appropriate matching jewelry and jewels on her high heel shoes. She competed in the ball-gown competition and won, probably because they could see her lipstick from afar. By the end of the night she had quite an impressive set of lips on her.

I didn't bring the camera. Cindy and I still love to recall this story and torture Jennifer. And Jennifer is still appreciative of her bosom of the evening.

That is my finest example of a woman doing anything to attain the fashion look she wants to wear. She suffered that truss of tape for 12 hours, until three in the morning. She rejected pale lips. She strutted and danced and stuck out like a fancy blue plumed bird with a red beak.

Of course when the time came, the duct tape didn't come off easy, and had its pound of flesh—well at least some of the top layer of skin. She started screeching then—but it was brave screeching. She never voiced any regret over the make-over of her chest. Without complaint she treated the skin peeling and chapping for a week or more. Regardless, to her, the pain was worth the price that for once in a lifetime, she had cleavage to go with her blue costume and red mouth. (Yes, she danced a lot more than Cindy and me, and met a new guy. We, dressed as Dorothy and Toto, and did not.)

So if you're looking for cleavage, I can fix you up.

# 7.

# Solo on Kepler Lake

This is a small, personal trip. I'm glad the grass, moss, and bushes are still variants of green, but it will soon go brown or be covered with early snow. Sometimes winter comes too darn early. Fall is knocking, opening the door as I drive down the highway to a little lake that doesn't get much attention.

Kepler Lake is part state park, and part rental lease. I pull into one of the three tilted spaces for the state park and wrestle the little canoe from the top of my little car. There are usually two of us and I didn't plan ahead for a solo canoe lift. For a moment I pause, sweaty, having scratched the paint on the roof, and wonder: why am I doing this? I'll never get that canoe back on top. But now it's down, and I am committed to seeking the peace of the lake.

I pull on my hat and fingerless gloves, and button my down jacket. My boots feel clunky in the shell of this canoe. An occasional fish comes to the top and sends rings out on the quiet water.

There is a small bridge with access to the side of the parking lot. I aim the canoe into the settled and clear waters at the other end of Kepler Lake. The bottom of the green lake has some grass and sticks in its sand. Sometimes, in the summer, it is churned up by too many people fishing and swimming. Now I have the place to myself. I feel like I'm in a golden cathedral, that I shouldn't make too much noise or disturb this small lake nested in the forest.

I cast my line and bring my spinning Mepps lure back to the canoe. Dark green shadows move under the water in their navigation around the lake. They aren't interested in my lure right now. The trout will bump the lure, but they will not take it into their mouths. Maybe they're smarter than we think. Sometimes one doesn't have to fish to justify being on a lake in a canoe.

The weaker sun has a lateral slant this time of year that causes the light to do strange things, and cast long shadows. It will drop over the northwest corner of the lake. It is silent. The rare kind of silent that almost rings in ones ears. The hands on the water are calm.

It's a pleasure to glide the still waters, and it does restore my soul. The smell of the water holds just a tinge of silver fish scales, and in the air a hint of spruce and turning leaves. It's so quiet it causes me to think about being alone in the lessening light. How it might not be the smartest thing one could do—go off without telling anyone. From here, one could believe they were a hundred miles from nowhere, rather than about 15 minutes from Wasilla, less to Palmer.

Having a small private lake to myself, I tour the shore, the edges of the water and pause at a shushing creek that is feeding the lake. Some willow branches lean into the water. I pass over snaggy branches at the bottom of this shallow lake. Why don't I do this more often? Probably because I'm not that good with a canoe. But the fish and the trees don't care. Birch are still holding some of their golden leaves, and they sprinkle gold ornaments that catch in the spruce. There is an unending cycle of fish making the rounds of the figure 8 shaped lake.

The intoxicating silver-fish smell of the lake, and cranberries, and decay—there are no good words for it—keeps me paddling until my fingers are stiff with cold, my knees creak like rusty hinges, and my eyes are open too wide with trying to see in the coming darkness. Peace prevails.

I pull ashore, and stretch, and eye the canoe. I get my keys, and wonder how I am going to get that canoe back on top of the car by myself. I'm parked on a steep slant. It is getting hard to see. Then, like an angel, headlights cut the solitude, bounce down the potholed drive, and a Bronco pulls up beside me. Willing to help without being asked, two men lift the canoe like it is a feather, and I don't have to do anything but watch, and then tie it down.

They easily remove their own canoe, and by now, the fish will probably decide to take the hook. It's the right time of day.

I pour coffee from my thermos, and eat a couple Fig Newtons. On the way home, with the heater on full blast, I rub my cold hands, and I try to keep some of the hangover feeling of the peace I experienced. Why don't I do this more often?

8.

# Motor Home Reality

All those commercials and photos of merry motor-homers are a set-up. A motorhome is a tin and plastic shoe box of screws and pumps and drawers and tanks. There is no such thing as a trip in a motorhome where everything goes right. You love your motorhome in spite of its many, many flaws—but no trip ever happens without something breaking, or bending, or freezing. It may be as little as a dent, or a hose or a dead battery, or a bed that won't fold out. It may be the catalytic converter. It may be the plumbing/pumping system. It may be a crack in the black water tank.

Maybe those guys with hundreds of thousands of dollars in their rolling gold baskets have better luck. But, somehow I doubt it.

This is the real story of motorhome travel:

It was May, and the cleanup of the Exxon Valdez was in full swing. A business trip doesn't usually include a motorhome, but every bed was filled in the town of Valdez. Steve, Sue, and Janet took a rented motorhome, Ralley Econoline (R.E.), from Anchorage to Valdez and ended up parking in a little gravel turn in the road.

Our business concluded late Friday, and we elected to stay over because Valdez to Anchorage is a seven hour drive in a motorhome.

As our group packed up our things on Saturday morning there was not a cloud in the sky, and Valdez showed us her best. At the Chevron station (never pass a gas station in a motorhome in Alaska) we stocked up on barbeque and chili corn nuts. Then we stopped at Rich and Fred's to say goodbye.

After a leisurely breakfast we headed out of town and up Thompson Pass. (Thompson pass is a notably narrow, steep, and high risk pass in any but the best weather.) Free of the encumberments of work we happily stopped at Bridal Veil Falls and captured pictures of a waterfall rainbow in the sunlight.

We had no reason to expect that we were heading into the Twilight Zone. We made it to highway mile 15, which is 15 miles out of Valdez, and it was marked by a rusty snowplow pole/marker hanging over the road. It was then that R.E. (the motorhome) started bucking like a stuck horse. Soon we were dead in the water in the passing lane after having bucked past a pull-out that Sue had observed for Steve about 13 times.

To Sue and Janet's quiet amazement, Steve rolled the motorhome backward in an effort to make a three-point-turn so we could aim back toward Valdez. R.E. decided to come to a rest straddling all three lanes. So—Sue and Janet got out to push. The gravel was the only rolling thing on the road, a beat-up Blazer approached. It was leaking liquid like a sieve. Still, help had arrived in the form of a tiny woman. Right behind her a man who was bicycling the pass stopped to offer assistance too. We all put our muscles to the back bumper, and R.E. finally gave in and turned back down the pass.

Still no ignition, and no choice, Steve coasted R.E. back down the mountain for miles. We passed some trucks in the steep parts, they passed us in the not-so-steep parts. After a few miles we past the man on the bicycle and waved.

Steve tried the ignition, and R.E. came to life. It had to be a bubble in the gas line. Steve decided we should give R.E. one more chance and turned us back up the pass. We drove back to Bridal Veil Falls. Back up the pass, past the falls, back to the rusty yard arm, where R.E. started bucking again like there was a radio signal to the engine, and it once again died.

Steve coasted backward in another attempt to make a three point turn in a motorhome with no power. This time Steve, Sue, and Janet pushed with all their might and the RV once again coasted down the pass, back past the guy on the bicycle. After about ten miles, the same spot as before, R.E. started again. This time we drove back to Valdez and Big Wheel Automotive Center and Tire Repair.

There, Tall Paul looked under the hood and told Steve to remove the inside skirt and engine cover because he needed to go in through the inside. (This is not something anyone wants to do.) Steve removed approximately 20 screws, and a huge plastic hump-like engine cover. Then he went to make some phone calls. Cell phones were just coming into mass popularity and didn't get coverage in this area. That meant finding a pay phone and/or someone who trusted another with his phone—because calls cost money then.

Dust from the Big Wheel parking lot filtered in as people tore through the lot in some kind of race across the unforgiving dirt and holes.

Our bicyclist friend came by to check on us after setting up his camp. He seemed fresh and rested. We could see pity in his eyes.

Paul and Steve came and went. Dust sifted in on us. We waited. And waited. Some laborers got off work and gathered their trucks to drink their beer at Big Wheel. They went home. Steve went to make some more calls. Sue made coffee. After a while, Paul wandered back and decided he could go at the engine from under the hood.

We wrestled the engine cover back in place, and Steve put back the 20 reluctant screws that held it in place.

After a while Paul came back and had Steve turn the ignition off and on 108 times. Then he left for a while again. Steve went to make some calls. Paul sent for a new gas filter. After a while the filter arrived, was installed, and we were on our way.

We had decided on an alternate plan of pulling into a Blueberry Park, sixty miles up the road, and fixing a late dinner and restarting in the morning.

We relaxed this time as R.E. drove up the pass. At the rusted yard arm R.E. picked up some signal from outer space, choked again, and died. This time Steve caught the RV mid buck, we were facing back down the hill but sitting in a flat spot.

Sue and Janet bravely waved as Steve set out to find a phone in a land where few men roam.

After another pot of coffee, and no sign of Steve, Sue and Janet began to worry that Steve had been killed by some crazed trapper who shot him for wearing a red work coat that could be from the Exxon team. Finally, Sue tried a special combination of toe tap on the gas and hitting the ignition switch while we sang the words to: *on the road again*. R.E. started. Sue and Janet went in search of Steve.

Steve had walked to an accumulation of dead cars and little buildings and trailers. It turned out that the main trailer housed nine kids watching TV and taking turns talking to someone on the phone in Fairbanks. (Remember, no cell phones.) Steve sat down and watched the Dolly Pardon/Willy Nelson concert with them. After the concert was over, and everyone was done on the phone, they let him use the phone.

He came out the dingle-berry deep woods drive as we backed up and down the road in search of him. The sun was starting to set and it was about 10PM, as we pulled into what we now affectionately called into Big Wheel. Paul asked Steve to turn the ignition 40 or 50 times and said: you may as well park it for the night.

Sue's dream of a campfire and grilled salmon were smothered in the auto parking lot. Steve made some phone calls. Steve, Sue, and Janet set off toward Pizza Palace wondering if they still served at 10:30pm. Steve carefully hit every pot hole along the way.

Then Sue spotted a side road by the airport. It led to a beautiful little spot just waiting for homesick R.E. Not ones to say we should sleep in a noisy, dirty, dusty wrecking yard on the busiest highway in the state, we parked at our special spot. Steve started a fire, bats flew over the campsite, neighbors and dogs howled, and Sue grilled salmon and potatoes. Never did a camping dinner taste better.

A couple of bottles of red wine later we all retreated to our bunks. It didn't even matter that the pillows were rocky and flat.

At the crack of 9AM, Steve had showered and shaved, and he aimed R.E. and two ruffled looking women back toward Big Wheel. Paul said he would be right out to work on the RV. Steve left to make some phone calls.

Janet and Sue had time to shower, make coffee, and eat the ends of the French bread. Paul and Steve returned. After a few minutes of tinkering Paul essentially said: you're on your own.

At 11:45am on Sunday we headed back up the pass. The falls had lost their cachet. Janet and Sue were grimly strapped into different seats than the last three passes at the pass.

But as we passed the rusty yard arm, a collective sigh was released. No bucking bronco. Paul had fixed the problem. We would get back to Anchorage by evening.

At mile 25 R.E. bucked, kicked and died. Determined not to unpack this motorhome full of gear in Valdez, Steve manhandled the RV to the top of the pass and coasted down the other side. It soon became uncomfortably clear to Sue and Janet that Steve intended to nurse R.E. back to Anchorage. We were in the back of nowhere, and it was unsettling to think of being stuck without resources, in particular food.

It was then that we all came to the terms that we would drive like heck for 30 minutes, R.E. would die, we would pull to the side of the road and make a pot of coffee and add some Bailey's and eat some corn nuts. After a bit, R.E. would start and we would go another 30 miles—all the way back to Anchorage.

Forty miles before Glennallen, we coasted into a general store. Steve told the woman store owner about R.E.'s problem. She gave him a jug of Kingston rubbing alcohol to add to the tank. We were no longer concerned about being held responsible for damage to the RV. R.E. started and we made it to Glennallen where gas prices were eye watering. He added a couple of bottles of Heat to the fuel. The girl who checked the oil bent the hood latch so the hood would pop up the rest of the trip. She also kept the gas cap. But R.E. was running like a champ.

We no longer panicked at the 30 minute deadline. We didn't care that the hood latch clicked up and down. It was then a new problem appeared. Steve would not pull over, and drove past all eating establishments. He'd have another diet Coke and some corn nuts and tell us: that one was closed. That one isn't clean enough. I don't think they have a phone.

It was now 3:30pm and Sue and Janet hadn't eaten anything but French bread crusts, corn nuts (which get old fast) and coffee. Steve barreled R.E. down the highway, pedal to the metal, bouncing from frost heave to frost heave. Coffee no longer had any appeal.

During our trip we had seen bear, moose, caribou, porcupine, and rabbits. On the other side of Glennallen the Easter Bunny lost all sense of judgment and ran out, and you know R.E. doesn't maneuver well. We felt a thump and looked back. We told ourselves that the bunny did not know what hit him. But it was still depressing, another chink in the day.

More than six hours after leaving Valdez another restaurant beamed on the horizon. Steve intended to pass by, but Sue threatened to hit him so hard he would spin around twice before he hit the ground. Then he realized he had only one diet Coke left, the corn nuts were gone, and he could use a phone. So, we stopped at Eureka Road House. Steve went to make phone calls. Janet and Sue snatched the menus from the waitress' hands.

Once Steve got in the swing of stopping he wanting to stop at all the restaurants along the next 100 miles. We had apple and cherry pie with ice cream at Long Rifle Lodge. Steve went to stop again and Sue threatened him again. It was time to go home. Like an old horse heading for the barn we steamed into Anchorage at 8:30pm. We complained and cleaned out the motorhome. Monday morning was going to come early, and we'd been shaken and bumped and tossed and starved and dusted and aggravated in the motorhome for three days and two nights. Never, never, never again.

Steve bought himself a motorhome the next week. There's something about a box with wheels, beds, a refrigerator, and toilet and the open road. It just goes so well with the strange roads of Alaska, when the engine runs.

I'm pretty sure that Steve and the Exxon Valdez were the tipping point on cell phones. But cell phones still don't work in Thompson Pass. Up a hill and down a hill. Up a hill and down a hill. It's lonesome out there.

# 9.

# Cranberry Moose

Fall was fully upon us and the decaying leaves smelled like dirty sweat socks run through a fresh air filter. To Alaskans it is refreshing—to people not from here, they suspect a wet dog has been in your house or car. It's time to pick low-bush cranberries. Low means low. The berries are generally no further off the ground than two inches. They are the size of green peas, and gleam like rubies in the sun. It takes a lot to be meaningful—which means enough to make cranberry liqueur—a half to whole gallon of berries. I ignore my back pain in order to hunt and gather. Or sometimes I just sit down in the patch.

Except, when I went to my baseline berry patch, and there was not one berry. I went to the next patch, two berries. I should have had about two cups by then. The cranberries had let me down this year. I would have accused the moose of Hoovering them off if there had been a scattering of berries here and there.

I stood in the middle of a fruitless patch, wondering if cranberries decide to take certain years off. The mosses were deep green and spongy, the mushrooms were brilliant orange with white spots, and everything looked like it should. So, where were the berries? I also wondered how I would provide low bush cranberry liqueur as it was awaited by friends.

Then, I heard a rhythmic, soft, slightly crunchy step. This is a heads-up sound where we live. I glimpsed what I thought was a person on the road and continued to stack up a few windfall branches. Then I saw a moose head. And two smaller moose heads. Not good.

It's not good to be standing around a momma moose and her two calves. Moose can be as dangerous as bears when protecting their young. We have a place on our property that we call the moose nest. It's at the top of a hill, and it's where we piled some of our winter-kill trees and branches. They think this is their property, their delivery room, and have the willow and birch all staked out.

Nothing makes a body more nervous that one or two baby moose toddling around, mixing up their legs, and crying for their momma. They are precious and so vulnerable. Thankfully, these calves had had the summer to put on some growth. Still, mom-moose is never far away. They were all too close now.

Our 'yard' is wild and without benefit of any lawn or flat land. I was up to my ankles in rolls of moss, spruce windfall, tippy tussocks, and big, old downed trees. I was not close to the house.

Instantly, as my ears and eyes clicked on the moose, I became loud (the recommended tactic) and nimble. I looked over my shoulder to see a moose cow and two calves at the top of the drive. One feels very small when near a moose. And running through tree rutted, bush and spruce studded land does not make for grace. More likely a broken ankle. It felt like it took a long, long time to get to the deck. I was wobbly by the time I got there—but felt safe being up a set of stairs and in the confines of the deck railing.

It had been a good, green summer and they all had thick coats and a nice layer of fat on the back. I had their permission to watch from the deck. No matter how many times I see these animals, I am still in awe. I am still respectful.

I always leave all my doors open when I'm outside. Too many times I've looked up to see a moose or a bear nearby. We thought about putting a park-like walk around the property, except we have a couple moose and bear thoroughfares that get steady use. Out on such a trail there'd be no place to get out of the way.

I try to hold back the forest as it tries to crowd in next to the house. Like most people. I enjoy a bit of yard work. In one of my attempts to tame the land I was alone, I fell and hit my head on a rock. It knocked me out and I had to crawl back to the closest door. The house can't be seen from the road. Now, an open door, and a phone, are basic safety tools. It would be so hard to protect one's self with a gun—these animals don't just drop unless you have perfect aim at the perfect spot.

My total take of berries that day was five. I yielded the willow and grasses to the moose, and watched them from the deck—with the door wide open behind me. They daintily stepped through the bushes and moss, and thrashed their favorite bushes and trees. The moose grew up here and I respect their right to terrorize me.

## 10.
# Earthquake Day

First it sounds like a train pounding up a hill in a tunnel. There is no tunnel or train. Then the floor slides sideways, the windows begin to flex, and the hanging lights start to sway. At that moment, every Alaskan heart stops and we all wonder: is this finally the BIG ONE?

When we have a quake in the middle of the night I always think: we can't have the BIG ONE now, I'm too tired. Like it matters how I feel to mother earth.

Thursday's earthquake was as close as I want to come to the BIG ONE. This shaking and cracking went on and on. Then the ground snapped hard like a giant rug being shaken out. It seems to be common to freeze where ever one is, whatever one is doing, during these moments, waiting to see if there's going to be a throw-down, so to speak. So I sat there waiting for the dishes to fall out of the cupboards.

It seems like the earth is sliding and snapping under one for a very long time. The quake was over 6.1, and lasted forever. Well, maybe two long minutes. Just watch the clock for two minutes and see how slow it goes. Anything over 6 on the Richter Scale is significant. Our home was built with earthquakes in mind—that doesn't mean we don't experience cracks in the sheetrock, and broken seals in the windows. We accept this like we accept cracked windshields as an Alaska way of life.

Our hope, after these quakes, is that what just happened was a geologic and seismic equivalent of letting off steam—the *several small quakes are better than one gigantic quake' theory*. At least we all had something to text about on a quiet day. It is surprising how long the lamps keep swinging, and the aftershocks roll under the house for hours afterword. Probably no feeling can be more fundamentally wrong and disorientating than having the earth move under ones feet. Earth is not supposed to do that.

## 11.
# Road Trip from the Top of the World

Have you ever wanted to drive the Trans-Alaska Trans-Canada Highway, in a motorhome, between Alaska and the Lower 48? Or would you like to do it again?

*The Alaska Highway would be impossible to create in eight months today. Alaska currently does not have highways to the Alaska Peninsula, or the entire west coast of the state. Folk are dependent on flying, however expensive it may be. Presently, the permitting, and road plan, and safety and environmental regulations would stick it in political glue similar to the various bridges and roads that are analyzed for dozens and dozens of years. This is similar to the Trans-Alaska Gas Line, which has failed to go forward since 1976, in a world and a country dependent on energy resources.*

*In 1942 US Army Engineers pushed toward each other from Canada and from Alaska to meet in the middle, 1,500 miles, and provide a route for supplies needed to strengthen military defense during WWII. The builders faced skyscraper mountain peaks, dense clouds of mosquitoes, nasty white socks flies, bogs, and a variance from 100 degrees above* zero, to 50 degrees below zero. Many hard workers died from construction accidents, and exposure. Talk about inhospitable. The highway has been under construction since then.

Our Alaska motorhome is not one of those pretty silver and black bus-type units with automatic levelers, a microwave, a TV, or granite counter tops. Ours was made to take to the beach and the woods, without panic about ruining ones vacation investment. In fact, the inside is mauve and oak. That tells you all you need to know. But I have the greatest travel memories from the Mallard. Most important, we are able to take our dogs with us nearly everywhere.

The lure of the open road, in my own little house on wheels, definitely calls to me still. In taking the Alaska Canada Highway, we would be driving one of the most diverse, unpopulated, spectacular, textural cross sections of nature in the world. It is guaranteed to make one wonder at our smallness and fragility—and at geologic history.

## Extracts from Motorhome Log:

Departure: Anchorage
Janet's Entry, August 27, Friday

The kids promised to take good care of our geriatric dogs, and the house. I'm not totally confident. I will be calling them. *[The dogs survived, the house was burgled, and they forgot to open the damper on the fireplace and smoked the house. The trash was loyally still in place. Other than that, everything was fine.]*

After work, and some last minute packing, we departed in a frenzy from Anchorage, Alaska, in our new-to-us Mallard motorhome. We didn't yet know how often things would fall in the coach, fall off the coach, and slam open on rough roads. Not quite prepared, it seemed important to get started regardless. We had two weeks to drive down to Idaho, and fly back to Anchorage.

Just before we left, in the garage we smelled down a trace of very scary odor and realized one of the kids had unplugged the box freezer to plug in a tool, and hadn't plugged the freezer plug back in. The worst smell and clean-up ever. We didn't have time to get furious.

For those of you who have never had a freezer melt-down, you'll find a cloth over your nose and mouth is necessary. Retching, Dick reached over and plugged in the freezer—a brilliant move that would allow us to deal with frozen, putrefied fish when we got back.

It was so freeing to pull out on the road and leave behind the freezer, our jobs, and family/friend worries. The worry-free part lasted about 4 minutes, until the motorhome engine started a loud growl. Engine problems before a 2600 mile trip over a distinctly unpopulated terrain, a road renowned for its curves, gravel, steep mountainous runs, cliffs, pot holes, and construction—yay. Still, it was a dream of mine.

Dick decided to push on through our rumbling engine noise and see what happened. I was mentally percolated and committed to a long-planned two-week trip, and I wouldn't let a little knocking stop me… Pulling out of town we looked back at the purple and blue sunset. We made it to the Matanuska Valley Campground. Suddenly, we realized summer was over and that it was dark at night again.

The change in light doesn't happen overnight—but it seems like it. We're used to never needing a light turned on—then we go to needing lights in the morning and evening.

Dick's Entry August 27

Our beginning mileage is 29,304. Four minutes on the highway and the motorhome suddenly begins to make a high pitched "buzzing" noise; as we slowed down the volume decreased. We pulled off at the Polar Theatre to check it out.

With the engine in idle, no noise; we get back on the highway and the noise picks up at 45 mph and increases with speed. So much for the tune-up. We debate whether to go on, or not, and decide to go. I hope we don't regret it. All other engine signs appear to be fine.

Our first night campsite surprised us. It got dark! We were near a stream and backed up to Mat-Su Glacier. Very quiet. Not many campers this time of year which suits us fine. In the morning we took a little time to reorganize the motorhome, something we would do many times.

Check the gas, water, battery, oil, leveling blocks—pray the pumps all work. Hope that the engine would hold together for 2600 miles.

The latest Milepost is our highway bible describing the road mile by mile, listing every trail, body of water, and large rock. It's a must have for Alaska and Canada travel. It pinpoints areas with any services available (believe me, that's important), and the history of particular sites, and how the fishing is on any body of water.

Janet's Entry—August 28

Dick got up and pulled the window shades and said, "Look what happened last night! Fall!" We were just enough further north from Anchorage to be there for the first coloring frost. Gold, red, and orange leaves glowed like lights all up and down the steep mountain sides. We took a hike up to view the Matanuska Glacier—our first roadside diversion. Rose hips, raspberries', and cranberries' tang filled the air with their airy sweat-sox scent. A smell maybe only Alaskans can love.

After receiving strict instructions to stop at Sheep Mountain Lodge for pancakes, we did, and they were out. Breakfast was good anyway. We have graduated to sweatshirt weather.

At the hub, Glennallen, we made our first stop (among hundreds, it seems) for gas, and then road construction. By the time we reached Tok, we had experienced many construction stops and much sticky road, our brown and white motorhome was covered with mud from the top rails, to its toes. I was used to having it washed.

Tok is 93 miles from the Canadian border, and came to life during the building of the Alaska Canada Highway. Tok is big enough to be a pit-stop for highway drivers.

I'm sort of embarrassed to this day, because I had hoped the construction would stop there, (on the way down the highway?!) and shared that hope with the carwash attendant. We washed the motorhome and went for gas.

The gas station owner said: Lady, are you kidding? It won't do any good to wash it till you get to the states. Understatement.

As we took up the road again, we started to wonder if the truck's shocks would last to Idaho. The road was so rough it was a little like riding a camel. Nature turned out in a full pallet of colors including neon. The trees had just turned yellow, gold, green, peach, and orange and were backlit by the sun. The fireweed, berries, and grasses had turned every color of the fire gradation.

As the sun dropped low and cast a vertical light it was about 9pm. Colors went neon bright. The distant mountains scanned an array of purple colors, and the moon advanced. We passed a beaver pond with three still industrious beaver still working their dam.

We started off the trip kind-of backward, leaving late, and driving late, and because we could, we continued that pattern.

Dick's entry August 28

On occasion we spotted the Trans-Alaska Pipeline. It raises far enough off the ground to accommodate wildlife passing underneath. It seems immaculate and we wonder at 800 miles of pipe crossing these wild, towering mountain ranges and valleys, and constructing it until they got to Prudhoe Bay.

The drive was a day of contrasts; some of the most beautiful scenery on earth accessed by the worst *highway* I have ever traveled! The road from Sheep Mountain to Tok is bad, then it improves from Tok to the Border, then look out!

The truck got quite a beating; I think the exhaust manifold gaskets are blown again. We won't even discuss the alignment. Janet bought six rolls of film; now she wonders if we'll have enough! At one point we stopped three times in fifteen minutes. Black bears, beavers, sheep, and porcupine were some of the wildlife of the day.

We (I) decided to press on to White River for the night; with the late start and miserable road it was too far. It's good to have a bed with you. Still, we found a generous camp spot sitting on a river. One could not have ordered up a more exotic, colorful, remote site.

Janet's Entry - August 29

Just as the <u>Milepost</u> promised, after Kluane, the roads got better. The views never disappointed. It was a little like trying to get a drink of water from a fire hose—too much glory to take in. The road allowed us to drive for some time just a few feet from the shores of Lake Kluane. The lake's color is that impossible blue, green. We stopped for lunch, and I needed to look for driftwood. There was some seriously beautiful, bleached driftwood, but Dick was not into having me tie it to the top of the motorhome. I did bring one piece, maybe two.

Lake Kluane is a long lake and it was a pleasure to be able to drive next to its aqua waters for many miles. We haven't seen another vehicle for a while. This is the very definition of an *emerald wilderness* staggering with layers of rock, with a narrow road meandering through it.

Note: It was my birthday. After seeing several tantalizing signs, we were excited about stopping at China Garden in Whitehorse, in the Yukon Territory for dinner. White Horse is a pretty little mountain town with a bit of European flavor, and the diagonal street parking of the old west.

We had passed the White Horse exit the first time, expecting to be lead through the middle of the town, and had to turn around and go back.

We were looking forward to *"the best Chinese food above the 60$^{th}$ parallel."* The waitress met us at the door, frowned, and wouldn't give us menus. She pointed toward the Chinese buffet-smorgasbord. The restaurant was multi-cultural with shamrocks, cowboy hats, Chinese artwork, paper lanterns, fifties Formica tables and chrome chairs, and a log reception desk. One wall was papered with glowing reviews of their food.

I made the mistake of asking for tea—in a Chinese restaurant. The waitress was very put out. Eventually, we got a pottery coffee pot and two heavy mugs and Lipton tea bags.

We didn't know we were early diners. The buffet was small and newly set up and we were given our assigned plates. We sat down with our tentative platters of food. We started off with hard rice and hard noodles. The ribs and chicken were good. We looked at the empty restaurant and chalked it up to typical road fare.

Harmonica and accordion music played in the background, laced with some Irish tunes and a little 50s crooning. Dick gave me my cards and gifts with as much ceremony as possible.

We blinked our eyes, and the place was full of people. Every table. People were backed up behind the buffet fiercely calculating how much food was left, and already calling for more. We heard people exclaiming how they had driven all day to come to this buffet, and they were going to get their fill. (Hard rice and noodles...) Reluctant to poke back into the now long line, since we'd already had some food, and the diners looked as if they didn't take kindly to strangers manhandling their buffet—it was hard not to get silly. It was a most colorful birthday meal that let us touch a spot of life above the 60$^{th}$ parallel.

We stopped that night at another Provincial campground—Squanga Lake, Yukon. It was said to have northern pike, grayling, whitefish, rainbow, and burbot. Dick spent a little time wetting a line.

There were many commercial RV parks with hook-ups right on the road. They generally ran full price. The Provincial campgrounds were immaculate, down a short way off the highway, picturesque and pristine, and half the price.

Once again we went to sleep in a sparsely filled campground with the sounds of a creek running into a lake.

Dick's Entry

Squanga Lake is beautiful but quite shallow for over 100 yards from shore, so it wasn't really fishable without a boat.

Janet wanted to bring all the driftwood from the shores of Lake Kluane. I had to do some fast talking. I told her to put down the camera, and step away from the driftwood. Our days were going by fast and we had a tougher schedule than we expected due to the roads.

Our gasoline legs were short, about 220 miles—so we had to plan ahead for gas stations or risk being caught in a stretch between them with no gas. Not something we want to experience. Gas was about double the US price. When you think of what it had to go through to get to these outposts, you can't gripe.

I continue to look for cell phone coverage.

Janet's Entry—August 30

Today we went through that notorious winding highway of post card fame. It's more like a semi-controlled rollercoaster ride. I made the mistake of using my arms as shock absorbers in our captains' chairs and was very sore.

It's less fall here than in the Yukon. We are temporarily driving back the season just as we were totally under the inspiration of autumn. These roads took us to very tops of high mountains, back to the bottom and swamp spruce, and then back to the top. There is an art to mountain driving in a motorhome. Long, steep hills take all the engine's effort, and the coach goes slower and slower, until the top.

Day one and two of our drive were more like driving in gravel pits with pot holes. This part of the road is full of relentless switchbacks and curves and ups and downs.

We decided to stay at *Liard Hot Springs* for the night. I had to persist to get Dick to pull over. He was looking at the miles we needed to cover. I wasn't.

It seems like boardwalks over water can never be long enough. This walk was a most satisfying distance through the dinosaur age. Boreal forests and hot springs and warm water marshes are disorienting in the far north. One can see fish that only live in warm water, and there were frogs! There are no frogs in the North! The plants, except for the spruce and cottonwood, were unrecognizable. The water was crystal clear with unusual mosses, and the smokes or steam from this and other hot pools drifted through the trees and up the mountains as if in a fantasy. Many plants exhibited pale pink and sunny yellow leaves.

The Alpha pool is very large and lined with rocks. The sides of the pool look as if a gardener had prepared them. Monkey face flowers and ferns sprouted and flowed from the edges of the pool.

Of course, there is the overpowering smell of rotten eggs—sulfur. The pool is so hot one has to get in slowly, and immediately feels the need for a nap. But once a person gets used to it it's hard to leave. There is a hotter Beta Pool, and we walked up to see it. It was far less populated, and too warm for us. People from all over the world, speaking many languages, were staged around these pools for their medicinal purposes—and a good hot-tub soak.

A mama and baby moose were strolling through the marsh as we walked back from our soak in the Alpha Hot Pool. One is generally quite uncomfortable in the presence of a cow and her calf. These two tip-toed through the water, ate a dripping wet snack, and didn't pay us any attention.

The Alpha pool felt spiritual, and other worldly. Like we were given a magical trip to another world. Sleep came deep and fast that night after a bowl of chicken noodle soup. I promised I would make a return journey to Liard Hot Springs and stay longer.

Dick's Entry—August 31

We stopped for lunch and a hike at Cranberry Falls. The falls have cut a deep bowl into the mountain of rock. Janet is in a picture-taking mood. Again, at one point we stopped three times in 15 minutes. We only have so much time to do this trip. I need to find cell phone coverage for work.

Rain at the end of the day, after our dip in the Alpha pool hot springs, made for perfect sleeping.

Liard is pronounced Lee-ard; it is Tagish Indian for trees, meaning cottonwood trees.

Janet's Entry—August 31

Our check marks for the day included mountain goats, black bear, and deer.

I couldn't resist a final morning walk at Liard Hot Springs. Little did we know what was ahead of us when we started this morning. The narrow, broken, snaking roads up mountains, down mountains, and back up mountains rarely saw us break 35 MPH. We hit our 8$^{th}$, 9$^{th}$, and 10$^{th}$ stops for construction and lead trucks. We gave oranges to the construction sign holders. Most of them were going to college.

At the same time, the lakes and rivers and mountains and valleys are a new kind of spectacular. The bucking-bronco roads wind up and down forever.

Muncho Lake is an amazing blue green due to copper and sediments in the water. The mountains folded like a stack of sheets that had tipped over. Mountainous piles of layers caused me to want to be a geologist and study the area. The young geologic rocks looked like giant sculptures. There was no place to stop looking. Summit Lake had an elevation of 4,250 feet.

Dick was getting crabby after about 5 hours driving at what could have been an amusement park ride.

Talk about driving through the Twilight Zone, one minute we were alone were in the wildest landscape. The next moment we were at Fort Nelson and the roads were straight and wide, the mountains more tame, and the hills started to roll instead of spike. The highway poured into the foothills of the Rocky Mountains, and then into flatter British Columbia farmland.

We were used to towns consisting of a cluster of buildings and heavy equipment collected around the gas pumps. Here we passed farms, oil rigs, and logging towns. Combat driving with truckers made me want to go back to the other side.

We stopped at Charlie's Lake Provincial Camp Ground. We have parked on a lake or a river every night. We have not met with blasting music, or litter, or crowded campsites at any stop.

Dick's Entry—August 31

This morning we took a walk back to the Alpha and Beta pools to get more pictures! Then the road started rough and deteriorated. It took five hard hours to go 190 miles. Ugh.

It was like pulling back into the real world to come into the town of Fort Nelson. I was able to make some business calls. We decided we deserved milkshakes as a reward for riding a rocking horse for so long. The milkshakes didn't come easy, but we prevailed.

I was able to make some long over-due calls from Fort Nelson.

After Fort Nelson, the road improved greatly, although it was heavily populated with trucks. At this point we were starting to go back into high traffic combat driving, but made 236 miles in the next five hours. It made Janet homesick for the lousy but unpopulated roads up to Fort Nelson. All in all, it was a long day.

Janet's Entry—September 1

We had our earliest get-up and emptied the tanks, got fresh water, and drove to Dawson Creek to do laundry.

We had the most wonderful breakfast at the Windsor Hotel. The café was spotless and decorated with early American, tuxedo black and white, trains, ballerinas, modern art, and more. Miss Manners would call it eclectic. I call it great food that I didn't have to cook.

Dick's Entry—September 1

After laundry, we went to "Mile 0" of the Alaska-Canada Highway and took pictures. Then we found a mall where Janet could find Canada's good pain medications for her back. We also bought a few groceries. Most all the common goods were familiar brands, but labeled in French.

Continuing toward Edmonton, the countryside is progressively developed for farming, and ranching, and there are many little towns. The traffic has picked up, especially large trucks. We left the season of fall behind us and drove back into late summer. Although, mornings and evenings are cool.

Janet scolds me for driving so hard, but we should be in Banff tomorrow, right on schedule, with all day Friday to enjoy the benefits of the city.

The price of gas drops as we head south into bigger cities and busier highways.

We had no further mechanical problems with the motorhome, it's just noisier than your average engine.

Janet's Entry Continued

I did some housekeeping in the motorhome while Dick did laundry. It is amazing how dusty things got on those roads. We brought a little vacuum and it's like playing house—clean-up was so fast and rewarding. Cluttering it up happens faster.

This part of the trip brought us through lots of good size towns. The roads are in very good shape and dominated by truckers who have no fear and follow no rules. The Canadians have lived up to their long standing reputation as awful drivers. Alaskan drivers are not exactly noted for their manners. Maybe it's a draw.

Dick and I caught site of a few motorhomes heading for the Highway, waving to them with some envy, and some smugness. Envy for the untamed and unpopulated beauty—smugness that we've done that trail they call a road and they don't know what a spine jostling herky-jerky stop and go trip they're in for.

Some of the highway is dedicated to a Native Guide who helped mark it. Dick thinks he was getting even with the white intruders when he helped them blaze the snaking road.

I have to keep some reins on Dick—if it were up to him, we'd be in Coeur d'Alene tonight, and heading for Mexico tomorrow. He keeps asking me if I want to take a nap, because when I'm sleeping I can't make him stop. He is destination driven in a hypnotized kind of way.

Dick's Entry—September 2

After leaving the quiet, lovely campground we drove the last few miles of the "cut off" to Highway 16. We hoped we had the right road between Jasper and Edmonton. It seemed awfully lonely, no other vehicles, like before Fort Nelson. How far can someone go wrong in the middle of the Rocky Mountains of Canada? How much gas do you have? Where are the other trucks and motorhomes? We marched steadily closer to the Rockies wondering where exactly we were going in the middle of this huge country.

It turned out we had come to Jasper Park through a little used route that got a grunt from the gas station attendant. Hey. We made it,—sweating, and driving in on fumes. This happened a lot on this trip. We swore to have a gas rack put on the Mallard, for extra gas cans, but haven't yet.

Dall sheep cooperated by standing on the road to be photographed. It takes less time that way. We had lunch at Jasper and drove further into the park where we stopped to see a gorgeous waterfall. The glacial Athabasca River is light turquoise except the falls that are a furious, dashing white. The power of the falls shook the ground and the spray lent a surreal feel to our site seeing. Another hour took us into Banff Park. Janet now expects camp sites to include a water view.

Janet's Entry

I packed Keds and loafers, and forgot hiking shoes. My shoes are looking pretty tough at this point, and not at all appropriate to our hikes. Today we drove into summer. I put on cut-offs and then worried about blinding people with my Alaska tan.

It's easy to pick out the motorhomes that have been over the highway. They're the piggy ones with dust and mud and rock screens pocked with bugs. Many of them sport a bumper sticker that says, "I survived the top of the world highway," or "I survived the Alcan."

The park is full of teams of bicyclists intent on climbing every mountain. They staged out of vans, and were studiously taking the steep grades with pedal power. With mountain after mountain, some taking us as long as 30 minutes to reach one mountain top, we ground our way up steep pulls in the motorhome. We're not jealous of the biking teams. No one was smiling.

Today was another day of stunning scenery. The highways in Alberta all have been kept in very good condition. They have more money from farming, logging, and oil. They also have a LOT more people running around than in the Yukon. I guess my mind is still stuck back there. Camping was a dream.

We have learned how to keep things from flying around in the motorhome. We have a special routine for showers, water, meals, gas, and holding tanks. Maybe we should consider going to Mexico.

Motorhome rule: if you need it, it will rattle.

Motorhome rule: if you're at half-tank don't pass a gas station on the highway. (We sweated our way into a number of gas pumps before taking this to heart.)

We stopped and did our first bit of city tourist shopping in Jasper. It was fun for an hour—then time to move out of town again.

We saw two wild and wooly waterfalls today. The water pounds bowls and canyons in the rock carving other worldly sculpture. The glaciers here are interesting in that they exist at such a low parallel.

I never know what time it is. Our clocks have been wrong for days. It works in this case.

Tonight, I finally managed to spend some time with the water color pens and did a forest view, and a mountain view. Photos and art pale in the face of this textural tectonic country. And yes, we parked next to a river. I'm in love.

We headed into Banff, which has grown since I last saw it. It is no longer quaint. It is more sophisticated European and alpine. Loads of shops.

Dick bravely maneuvered the motorhome in heavy traffic on narrow streets. On my check list I had to take the gondola lift to the top of Banff's outstanding peak, up a sharply vertical grade hill. The ride skimmed the tops of spruce trees, people climbed the mountain under us. The hike averaged nine hours. It could be compared to climbing the roof of an A-frame house—only with rocks and trees on it. We were not tempted to walk. The view from the gondola was to forever, and we didn't break a sweat.

We hiked around at the top with a 365 degree view. In the friendly walking places on the top of the mountain, we went to inspect a preserved weather station cabin where they hiked in and out weekly with supplies; their duty was to watch for cosmic activity. Not for the un-fit.

Other languages floated around us as we sat on boulders to take in the view and took photos for other people. Squirrels started to press in on us. They wanted their nuts, now. At one point 7 squirrels had us surrounded and were closing in. Squirrels can be a little threatening. Like the movie The Birds, we felt as if we were being stalked. We had to leave. We didn't have any more nuts.

We had an expensive lunch of hotdogs and coffee on the open decks and watched people, the city of Banff, the smokes from hot springs, the castle hotel, and the mountains unfolding all around. We wanted to stay at one of the hot springs, but they all said: *full, or sorry*. This led us to keep going by the half hour for hours. We finally crossed the border between the USA and Canada at the Idaho border.

Dick's Entry

For the record, we arrived at Banff on schedule, no thanks to my wife. The drive through Jasper Park involved some of the longest hills yet. That's saying something. We saw a lot of people pushing their bicycles.

The ride up the mountain in the gondola lift was amazing. We got a car to ourselves, and could have almost reached out and touched the mountain. We finished up our film.

On to Cranbrook, a very long maybe-here, maybe-there, trip. Of course we had to run into one of those main roads that lead to nowhere for which Canada is famous. We headed for Radium Hot Springs to spend the night. It was full. We ended up driving another six hours in search of a hot spring. They were all full.

We stayed at a beautiful campground with the Kootenai River out our back door—making our camp sites perfect water sounds and views all the way down. We have the drill down to level the motorhome and get the beds ready, and to fold them back. It is handy to travel with a shower and a toilet in this wild country.

Janet's Entry—Saturday

This morning we headed down the tip of the Idaho Panhandle, and through blueberry berry-picking and hunting areas I hadn't seen since I was a child. We were back to the world of white pine, and jack pine, and the summer pine needle smells.

The towns are tiny and old. I don't know how people afford to live here. There is no industry larger than a bar. We pull through little square towns with brick buildings fronting Main Street—we spied a operating Mercantile. What would it be like to live here? One would always be a newcomer.

I felt shadowed by distant memories of this part of Idaho. Further down the road we neared Sandpoint, which had changed so much I hardly recognized what used to be one of my hangouts. I couldn't believe that K-Mart and Costco had settled in to what used to be such a small town. Lake Pend Oreille (*pond-der-ray*) was stunning as it always has been. We crossed the bridge over the lake on our way to Coeur d'Alene and saw many more businesses and homes. *Change* had arrived here. We got to my parents' place by about 1pm. For once I was not still exhausted and frazzled from work when I arrived there.

By 2pm Dick was having motorhome withdrawal and was ready to get back on the road. He and Dad started making plans to take the motorhome and go fishing the next day.

The overall plan was that the folk would take the motorhome to Arizona for the winter. That's another story.

Dick's Entry

I have wanted to see the panhandle of Idaho since Janet and I first came here. I can understand why Patrick McManus writes about almost failing school because of the lure of fishing and hunting in this beautiful, sparsely populated country of pine trees, lakes, streams, and blueberries. I wanted to come back here and fish.

We pull into Joyce and John's at about 12:30, ahead of schedule, thanks to Janet's marathon run of yesterday.

> Ending mileage: 31,922 miles Trip mileage: 2,618 miles and frequent stops for gas.

Dick's motto: Keep going. A rolling motorhome gathers bugs, but no moss.

Janet's motto: I need more film. (No we didn't have smart-phones yet.)

12.

# Golf Course Flasher

It was just a friendly game of golf, nine holes, with our woman's group on a sunny summer evening after work in Anchorage, Alaska. The sports skill level ranged from *me* to very skilled. There was the same old mumbling about slow players, and Canadian Geese sitting on the balls, mushy water features, and unfair sand traps. Big Bertha was hot on the scene and had become the go-to driver.

These golf matches were simultaneously competitive and talk therapy. Frustrations were taken out on the ball. Sue ordered us to spank that ball!

Our foursome was finishing up the 8th hole, the other of our foursomes was starting to set up for number nine, the last hole for the evening. I saw someone coming from the bushes at the edge of the golf course. I looked away and snapped back. He was wearing a red bandana over his face, and a tee shirt. He came strolling toward our two groups in hopes of—I don't know what. Trick or treat?

"There's a guy over here with no pants on!" I yelled.

"What!!!"

"We're being flashed!"

"There he is!" There was a stampede not away, but with golf clubs held high, running straight for our flasher.

Darla had her driver in the air and took off after him. Chris, also carrying a driver, dashed after him from the other side. One of our members had a golf cart and she went wheeling after him.

Some of us went thrashing through the bushes looking for our party boy. The cart made laps searching for our free thinker. No, we did not catch him. He must have figured that he picked a seriously unappreciative group to terrorize with his penis. We hoped he hurt himself running commando through the bushes.

High on our *fight rather than flight* reaction, we hurried back to the lounge and colorfully recounted his exposure and rapid retreat. What did his tee shirt say? Was he wearing shoes? What color was his hair? How fast did he run? How much did you see? It was the story of the night.

I can still envision the flasher, who was shocked by a marauding group of golf club wielding women who had no sense of fear about men flashing their foursomes, or whatever he wanted to call it. I have to admit, he must have been able to move fast when it counted.

The foursomes that didn't see him were distraught at being left out of the drama, and made us recount the experience over and over. It was just a friendly game of golf. And, a flasher who chose a marauding band of women who could have been wearing kilts and wielding swords.

13.

# Sears-Roebuck Woman

My job was to support and sometimes escort geologists and geophysicists around Alaska. How fun is that? It's the job of a lifetime. We went places no one else needed or had an excuse to go.

On one trip we were about to take, we would fly a visual survey, north, northwest. We wanted to speak to a Native Elder in Holitna, and check in at Sparrevohn AF military facility, on the wings of Alaska's work-horse plane, the red and white Twin Otter. (We were required to fly in a plane with two engines for insurance purposes.)

The plane was freshly lined with plywood and smelled woody like a tree lot. It was a snippy October morning and I was glad to have my down parka.

No pilot in Alaska takes flying Merrill Pass, north-northwest out of Anchorage, lightly. It sits above Anchorage, a sort-of gateway to the Alaska interior, and it has a reputation for being temperamental. It is a *gateway* because the Talkeetna and Alaska ranges are so tall and dense on either side of a deep valley.

We all knew this before we boarded the Twin Otter STOL (short takeoff and landing) Bush Plane. It was early winter in Alaska, and the sun came up about 9:30am, and went down about 6:30pm. It was early-season cold. As required by our company, all of us sported Arctic gear.—That means oversized, wrapped like a burrito, covering from head to knee coats.

Gear:
- Massive Knee length down parka with hood and ruff (looks a little like walking around in a sleeping bag)
- Down overalls, puffy and unflattering with whatever one decides to wear underneath (when you need them, you need them)
- Choice of down parka liner, usually with long underwear and a flannel shirt
- Felt-packed boots (the felt is ¾" thick), with wool socks (everyone has big feet)
- Oversized leather, long armed 'snot' mittens, native or military style
- In addition one has a bag or "gear" to hold various necessities, food, socks, thermoses, scarves, books, and overnight stuff

You either get *it* before climbing aboard, or before take-off. *It's* the weigh question. How much do you and your gear weigh? Everyone has to answer. And they have to be truthful. The pilots are rarely discreet and are not to be turned away by a coy female or male.

I was with a bunch of guys I had to work and associate with, and my weight has never been a number I felt the need to share. Fortunately, for this trip I had extra heavy gear. And, I had brought the traditional gift for remote Alaska: fresh apples, oranges, carrots, squash, and Halloween candy. Fresh fruits are prized year around because most planes that land in the villages are full of gear and people—not fruit. So I had to weigh them too. With my load, I weighed 260 pounds!

Why report one's weight? This is so the pilots can calculate the plane's weight for fuel, center of gravity, and cargo. This is particularly important for flying through Merrill Pass, which can be confounding. An overweight plane can be as dangerous as a missile in those skyscraper mountains.

I generally carried an Olympus SLR OM1 camera, but I forgot it, and felt naked without it. So, on this trip, I would watch the world through the window, and not the view finder and filters. It was a good mistake. A camera does not ever do justice to the sweeping views and the colors any time of year, and one can get so carried away with the photos as to miss the scene.

In these young mountains the pass follows through a long, narrow trench, and is armed on both sides by towering rock and snow-covered mountains. The wind hit the tops of the mountains causing low pressure in the lower pass. The temperatures can vary drastically across a very short distance. The pass has its own personal climate. Moist weather goes on to become rain or snow (adding the danger of icing) in the pass. The weather can be clear on top and terrible below. This makes for dicey flying. Why?

Cold currents of air buffeted the plane as if to discourage us from making this voyage. The wings dip between granite peaks, so steep and sharp that neither man nor ice can find rest on them. Some of the tallest mountains in the Alaska Range are the Talkeetnas. This means for the most part there are no good places to turn around.

There were ten seats in the plane in addition to pilot and co-pilot, and the four of us were strung out on each side of the cabin. No bathroom, no meal service, BYOS (bring your own snacks). Restroom: They pull a little flimsy fabric curtain at the back of the cabin and showed off a coffee can—if you're desperate for a toilet. Believe me, that would be desperate.

The geologic complexity of the pass had world-wise geologists and geophysicists shaking their heads as if to clear their eyes. They nod and hum their disbelief at what their eyes reveal. Light reflects off the shell of the plane tracing circles of pink, blue, and yellow on thin, low lying clouds. I wonder how it is possible that I am allowed to be let in on this experience.

In the creases between the mountains clear green water meets silty glacier water to make milky lakes. The shutter on the others 35mm cameras remind me I don't have my camera to capture this unique landscape.

Today we were heading to a small village with an airstrip near Red Devil. From there we will go to the Sparrevohn Air Force station, and return to Anchorage. It's an all-day outing.

It was a clear, frigid day. Good news for taking the pass. The walls of the plane radiated cold, and we had a couple hours to scour the uncommon landscape rolling out below us. The cold inside the cabin pressed through my parka. I'm sort of impressed, and sort of miserable when that happens. These coats are rated for far below zero. Twin Otters are not known for their great heating system. When it's cold through one of these parkas, it's cold.

Light airplane's heaters cannot generate enough heat to keep the plane warm inside. There is a base external low temperature point where the pilots won't fly. When you fly in cold weather, below zero, everything seems as creaky as a rusted bike, as untrustworthy as a crystal glass. It feels like the wings could simply snap off in a stiff breeze. These flights are not carefree. Pretty much ever. Yet, it wasn't that cold—more in the teen temperatures.

I brought along a thermos of coffee and one of cocoa. The passengers were happy to accept both, to go with their view of the pass.

Occasionally, one of us might spot the carcass of part of a plane hanging off a mountain, grim evidence that this pass was nothing to mess with.

High up in the mountains spires, circs look like an ice cream scoop gouged out the rocks, and the rocks, and shale looks primitive and unwelcoming. There are no foot trails here. There are no picturesque little cabins or caches. You are the fly darting around the room under a fierce fan blade.

We had some more coffee and cocoa.

The pilots seemed to visibly relax as we cleared the pass. We leave the mountains behind and cross over the Hoholitna River where the trees are not so skinny and stunted by cold. Ice is fighting to take over the river, and the tundra is sprinkled with its first snow. I couldn't help wonder if I could survive here. The world slowly became flat and white with connect-the-dot moose tracks, and sprouts of bushes and willow.

Survival thoughts were interrupted by a dab of civilization called Red Devil. It was the proud holder of the only liquor license and store for hundreds of miles. While happily consumed by many, alcohol is always a controversial subject in Alaska.

I believe all of us were looking forward to a toilet visit when we finally saw our landing strip. The strip was in good shape and the pilot dropped the Otter gently on to the snow-glazed gravel strip, which was not gentle. In a few minutes the local State Representative pulled up in his crew-cab pickup and we all piled in.

The geologists hoped to talk with local Native Elders and seek permission to overfly, or walk, and take rock samples on native lands the next summer. We bounce in fresh air bush-style to the family's lodge. I ask about the large airplane in the field next to the runway. The pilot said this plane had crashed here a few years back. The elder's son was wanting to make a house out of it, but hadn't gotten around to it yet.

The fruit we brought to the Chief had kids scurrying to grab it up and carry it away. We sat at a very large, thick, round table with heavy barrel-like chairs, probably homemade. The Elder's wife serves us instant coffee and powdered creamer so strong it does taste like the cliché battery acid—but we sip desperate to make a polite dent in the drink. By way of conversation with the geologic pros our host tells us that he had recently dug a well for water, that he hit bedrock, then water. It was a good well. They agreed that the Chief had probably hit a stringer of shale or sand.

I looked for bathroom accommodations, and they looked to be similar to those on the plane. I decided I could hold it.

We sip our coffee and admire the beaver hats the Chief's daughter made. The most die-hard anti-fur-folk would have to at least consider how warm these would be in the Arctic climate. They were for sale. I was hopeful for myself, but the price was way beyond my budget. The geologists bought several among them, and promptly put them on. Everyone was now happy.

I left my contact numbers and radio information with the Elder and asked what I could bring next time we came. He had to think about it. We returned to the plane, anxious sans bathroom break.

The Elder called to me as I reached the hatch of the plane and said, "I'll save my beaver skins for you, and next time you come you trade with me for Sears-Roebuck woman."

"Uh?" The guys are looking at me with lifted eyebrows and suppressed smiles.

The Chief said, "You know, Sears-Roebuck women, the ones in the slips and panties and bras?"

I didn't know they still made a catalogue. I did know about the underwear models. But, Sears probably didn't realize their catalogue substituted for girly magazines in the bush.

"All I want is Sears-Roebuck woman."

The guys asked me: "how would you manage that?"

I said: "you better hope I figure out something."

The guys happily talked about me finding a willing Sears-Roebuck woman as we flew on. The Elder didn't ask for me. Women in arctic gear do not appear to qualify as Sears-Roebuck women.

Still longing for a bathroom, we headed for Sparrevohn Air Force Station, a small military installation with radar. It seemed like it took a very long time to get to Sparrevohn. The landscape had lost some of its cachet and my eyes sought only a landing strip.

There it was! And there, as big and crashed as you please, was a C130 airplane carcass at the edge of the landing strip. With that grim hello, we landed. The strip was about two miles from the facilities. Once again we got off the plane and had to depend on the kindness of others. I crossed my legs. No one talked much. Apparently I had put a damper on free peeing, and there was nothing to hide behind. After all the Sears-Roebuck flack, I didn't tell the guys it was okay to wave their magic wands. I didn't want to suffer alone. After some time a vehicle came our way.

Our chariot was a rusted out old pick-up truck with no doors, and only a little bit of floor in the bed of the truck, and the cab. We all piled in, on, and over the truck for a brisk ride to the Quonset buildings. The traditional grated steps were stuffed with snow, and we stomped our feet in the accepted boot etiquette. The familiar sopping entrance rugs with tracks running two different pathways greeted us. The barracks and offices lead off one way. We only had eyes for the rec hall and the hope of a bathroom at last. Imagine the logistics of stripping Arctic gear down to go to the bathroom. We were grateful not to be trying to do this it outside behind a hummock of frozen grass.

The men met with the appropriate Air Force people, and I made several logistical phone/radio calls—the bane of my existence in the bush where a phone is a status symbol, works when it pleases, and is as rare as gold nuggets.

Before long, our pilots checked the weather again, and checked their charts, and checked the wind, and checked with Anchorage, and checked the weather. It was getting a little late for VFR flying. It turned out that Merrill Pass was not going to welcome us back through on this day. I admit that I was kind of relieved to spend the night somewhere warm and safe.

Sparrevohn AFB is a military infrastructure and support post for anyone in need in the middle of Alaska. There is radar and regular military facilities on a small scale. Even then, it seemed like these guys and I lived from one phone call to the next. I do not remember what was so important.

The barracks were barracks. I managed to find a spot on the other side of a wall, with good camping privacy. No mistake, these were very generous digs for an unscheduled overnight in the Alaska bush. We took turns with the bathroom.

A few of the men smoked pipes, and stories were shared, but all of us seemed grateful for a bed. The cold is very fatiguing.

In the morning I had to give my weight, less the fruit, in front of a dozen (mostly attractive) men. But at least I had my gear bag to protect me and my numbers. We climbed aboard the Twin Otter and returned through Merrill Pass. It was cold and clear and the plane cabin was cold and clear. We all seemed to take it light on the coffee and made a pit-stop before departing.

> *My Dad, a telephone lineman, was used to long sets in manholes, or the top of a pole. He made a four plus hour flight up to Anchorage from Idaho in a jet with no bathroom. He took his thermos and scheduled a cup of coffee on the hour. (He lived on coffee.) I practically held the door open for him when they landed, but he was fine—a veteran pacer.*

We flew over moose, their tracks as clear as polka dots. One can't help but be impressed by flying over and spying on a landscape few people will ever see. It's impossible to take it all in. I was convinced my camera would have helped. Finally, we landed safely in Anchorage.

I had recorded this unique trip in my mind, and not in my camera. I can still visualize it more clearly than other trips.

Political Incorrectness: When I got back to the office I sent my boss an email about requisitioning a Sears-Roebuck Woman.

Moral of the story: go to the restroom. Go right before you get on a small plane, and don't drink lots of liquids if you're going to be in the air for some time, and be sure of a toilet at your destination.

14.

# It's Good to Have Friends

Go gold mining! Love to.
My friends Joris and Regina had a gold mine operation in the Yukon. Miners are people of mystery. They never tell where their claims are. Claim-jumping is still alive and well and very serious. Alaskans know not to go wandering around aimlessly in gold mining country unless one doesn't mind an unpleasant encounter.

They decided to take a trip out to their lodge and mine. They leased a small jet, and there was happily a seat for me. Jet rides into the bush don't happen all that often, nor do trips to the Yukon and a gold mine. (Unless you're in one of the reality shows like *Gold Rush*.)

We flew from Anchorage to Dawson, Yukon Territory, over the clear skies of fall. The birch dominated the land with golden leaves like a plush rolling field. We flew over Lake Leberge (not many trees there) and had to recite Robert Service's: *There on a barge in Lake Leberge, I cremated Sam McGee*. It is an unremarkable but legendary lake, but also the location that inspired the poem famous to so many.

The jet landed in Dawson to clear customs. The terminal was attractive in a woodsy way, the tarmac in good condition, and most important, they had good bathrooms. The inspector who passed us through was a woman who wore a gold nugget necklace the size of a large man's thumb. It had a big diamond set in it. Her husband was a miner.

We toured the small, picturesque cemetery on the other side of the fence from the airport in Dawson. One head stone that said: *There are old pilots, and there are bold pilots, but there are no old bold pilots*. Another grave was headed by a propeller. Most of the headstones told an aviation story.

There we resumed our flight to a very modest, homemade airstrip near their lodge, Moose Lodge and Mine. There is always a moment of tension when landing on a gravel strip. The plane squirms.

Because of the rugged terrain it took nearly an hour to ride over rough roads, through golden birch, green and black spruce, and berry bushes. It looked like a path through the forest that could be almost anywhere in the north. It felt like a jungle rough ride to get to the lodge. Ptarmigan and rabbits hugged the side of the road.

We were going camping, right? This was no cabin. It was a full-sized, pristine, log lodge with traditional green trim. I really don't mind not roughing it, and was just fine with forgoing cots and cooking fires. The lodge sat facing a crystalline lake where tidy wooden stairs lead from the lodge to the water and dock. Gold leaves fluttered artfully about.

Moose Lodge had a large kitchen with two dishwashers and two refrigerators and two sinks. There was a separate bar, ice maker, ovens, and microwave, and any appliance one could think of. A generator hummed in the background providing all the power one could wish for.

The doors were all hand-crafted oak. The fireplace was built with local stone threaded with silver ore, and it was large enough to walk into. When they laid logs for a fire, they were real whole *logs* for a serious fire.

The carpet was a very deep green pile, and the traditional animal mounts were on the walls. The couch and wing back chairs were of burgundy leather and could have come from a lodge décor magazine.

On the front deck, overlooking the lake, was of course, a hot tub.

The beach was pebbly and covered with twisty, artsy driftwood. I wondered how much of it I could stick into my gear bag to take home.

There were three boats at the docks, and assorted utility buildings scattered here and there. I specifically do not name the nearby little town. I never actually saw the mine area. Four of us did do a little panning for gold and got a modest return (a few specks), bone-cold fingers, and creaking knees for our hours of sluicing.

When Joris, Regina, Joris' cousin, and I got back to the lodge, the caretaker had prepared for us (What? I'm not cooking!) grilled pork ribs, three kinds of fried potatoes, and a huge salad. After dinner the guys had cleaned the dishes in the kitchen, dancing to the music of the Rolling Stones. The sun set early on the lake.

The Yukon drink of the trip was Wisers' unblended Canadian whiskey, club soda, lime, and lots of ice. It grows on one. After dinner, the generator was turned off, and everyone sat in the silence of the Yukon, facing the fireplace, and telling stories.

The brothers who were at the lodge, had gone on a very recent hunting trip for Dahl sheep, got tangled up in the steep mountains and ended up in a canyon using their guns for walking sticks to climb out. They had hobbled their way back to camp, but their pilot and plane had failed to come back for them (every hunter's nightmare). Communications are notoriously spotty. They waited two days and were finally able to radio for a Twin Otter. It seemed funny—afterword.

The bedrooms were generous with big beds and down comforters. I felt like I was at a four-star lodge. The bathrooms had Jacuzzi tubs and showers. Can you imagine hot showers, and white down comforters in the bush? It's good.

The caretaker prepared (what?) a wonderful breakfast of English muffins, fried potatoes, eggs any style, juice, coffee, and homemade jam. The massive oak table sat a dozen, and with comings and goings, there were people siding up to the table at all times. Most of them were headed for the mining claim.

After breakfast the four of us took our fishing poles and lunch and headed out for the day. The family was helping to get the mining site ready to close for the season. (Once the ground freezes, mining goes from difficult to impossible.) We rode the jet boat out across the lake heading for a twisty shallow water area of connected ponds and many snags reaching up from the other side of the boat—pike fishing country.

The day was so clear and still that the trees, mountains, and skies reflected perfectly on the still water. We could have produced our own Yukon calendar. The air was crispy clean. We had worn the right gear for the trip—down jackets, fingerless gloves, boots, and hats.

The viewfinders of our cameras could not do justice to the place or the day. It was like something out of a coffee-table book. We had perfect pictures of fall in every direction with the slanted light of fall cutting brightly through the birch and cranberry leaves.

The pike were there, and would follow our Pixies and Mepps up to the boat, then swim away. We went ashore, hiked around, and picked fat rose hips and new pinecones, and searched for spruce-beetle-kill driftwood. (The dead spruce-beetle wood, without its bark, looks like someone carved a foreign language on the wood. Someone did, the spruce beetle.) We had fixed sandwiches and drinks, and sat in the boat and had a picnic and told more stories. The four of us were a long ways out from the lodge and it was time to head back.

Catching fish in Alaska is never a sure thing. The times one has the most confidence, one gets skunked. When one doubts the thrill of the day, they hit. And so it was with this trip.

On the way back across the lake the jet boat coughed and died. This seems to be a rule of boats, something written in their gear, something they must do on the way home. The guys changed the oil filter and we were back in business for a little while. We had traveled quite a way out and this was a big lake, and we hadn't made trip plans and left them at the lodge. So, sending for help was doubly tricky between the temperamental radio and our boondocks location.

Another rule of boats is that everyone has an opinion as to what is wrong. The boat drifted to shore and Regina and I cleared off a spot on the beach and built a big fire against the chill.

The guys got down with the engine, tried to call for tow, and then went to try and to blow out the fuel lines. We fed the fire and drank our thermos of spiked coffee. Soon, though, we were back in business and didn't need to be rescued.

We came back to a lovely turkey, accompanied with squash, mashed potatoes, gravy, broccoli, rice, stuffing and cranberry sauce. More than anything, I could have gotten used to having someone cook for me like this. That's luxury.

After dinner we all did dishes. Then the guys decided to rearrange the moose and caribou heads. Why? Because the *lips* on the caribou bothered them. So they defied gravity and moved the mounts. I watched, sure someone would break something personal. Tall ladders, heavy mounts, glasses of port, directions, and tipping antlers provided an evening's anxiety.

The fellows played a little poker and my friend and I turned in. I luxuriated in the soft bed after a full day, and enjoyed hearing the murmur of voices and the crack of the fire. The next morning was brilliantly sunny. The caretaker outdid himself with quail and ptarmigan breasts and fried potatoes and eggs.

Regina and I became trigger-happy photographers. Then, sadly, it was time to head back to Anchorage. What would it be like to spend a whole season here, not an option, a dream.

Before leaving, we went down and said goodbye to Moose Lodge and the lake, and boarded the van to take us back to the airstrip. The autumn angle of the light, the contrasts of the gold trees, and the Yukon spruce and pines with ragged mountains impressed even those who had seen it all before. The clarity and color of those millions of fluttering golden leaves bring an impossible light show.

Our group packed the jet full of bags and people and took off for Whitehorse under skies that were clear from the Beaufort Sea to the Cook Inlet.

Regina, a veteran flier got air sick. There was no turbulence. The further we got along, the worse she got. Finally it dawned on us that Regina was pregnant with their first child. So it was a landmark trip for Joris and Regina.

Dawson is a modern airport, and part of our gang got on a jet to go back to Calgary. The day was spotless as we flew back toward Anchorage, and over the glaciers and mountains of Kluane National Park, Yukon Territory, and crossed the border into Alaska.

Joris made good use of the pilot's maps and planned a once-in-a-lifetime extended tour over the southern glaciers and inlets. We passed over the area where Hubbard Glacier had closed Russell Fiord—it had moved up to 100 feet a day over the summer turning the fiord into a lake. Planes and helicopters were parked there with people who came to rescue seals and that had gotten cut off from the inlet.

Our jet flew past Mount St. Elias with an elevation of 18,008 feet. Malaspina Glacier looked like a horizon size order of chocolate and vanilla ice cream swirl spread flat across the main body of the glacier. The ice broke off the overhanging cliffs of the glaciers, and the ice dam would shortly break as proof of the power of nature. Our pilot took us over the port of Whittier and Portage on our way back into Anchorage.

## It's Good to Have Friends

We spent time at customs in Anchorage because we had failed to properly check out of Canada before entering Alaska. Another group was in the same holding area, and they had been there for 12 hours. I don't know what they did! So, we felt we got off light with a couple hours and a warning.

I did get to go back to Moose Lodge in the Yukon again with Joris and Regina and some friends. This time Joris and Regina took their daughter, and Regina was pregnant with their son. It was summer, and if you go by my experience, it's always sunny there.

# 15.

# Lime Village Camp

I'd never flown on a Caribou cargo plane. A huge hatch had dropped open from the back of the plane, just like the movies, and people began loading the many things we would need to set up a tent camp for ten people for eight weeks. Washer, dryer, refrigerator, tents of many sizes, food, radio equipment, wood to build the outhouse, and framing for the mess tent, a generator, oil, benches, heaters, and more.

It was awesome to see how much they could get in that tractor-trailer of the sky. The wing span was massive in order to carry the load.

My flight seat was a sling placed up close to the pilots, and my oxygen came from a bottle. I had no windows except the pilots' view. The mass of supplies was stacked up tight behind me. I always had good pilots who were willing to answer my many questions about the terrain and the plane. Alaska's bush pilots are a capable and proud few. Most people are in awe of bush pilots. There is good reason for that.

I repeat the saying: there are old pilots and bold pilots but no old, bold pilots.

We took off from Anchorage and headed to central Alaska's Lime Village, going through Merrill Pass. A ground-work geological field survey was being done there, which means most of the survey was topical. Some cores samples, rocks, and fossils were gathered from an area that had not been explored. My job was to help set up the camp.

Merrill Pass, (tricky all seasons of the year), was the best route to fly to the camp. The mountains on each side of this pass were so tall that it created its own weather situation in the pass. Glacier after glacier presented themselves, some covered with mud and dirt, others were that unique glacial blue. It was 75 degrees when we left Anchorage, and we were heading to a place where weather changes from 40 to 90 degrees faster than one can change their mind.

As the pilot aimed us toward a tiny air strip with spruce trees down the side, the pilot informed me that his wing-span was just inches under the width of the strip, and he had 6,000 feet to stop this behemoth. In other words, we were going to thread the needle. I never got used to landing on these tiny airstrips. It looked impossible, but the landing was perfect, the trees were indeed a few feet off each wing, and we arrived in a cloud of dust, and among fans cheering for the pilot. He was the classic bush pilot, and this was his world.

In Lime Village the weather could change in 15 minute increments—from cold and winds, to bright and hot, to hail, and back to hot many times over a day. The weather comes over the mountains from the Bearing Sea, and in July and August high temperatures (nineties plus), low temperatures (freezing), and hail storms are changelings to be respected.

Layers of clothes were constantly coming off and going on, which wasn't the worst part. Keeping every eyelash level of skin covered with bug dope was.

We don't have snakes or alligators or roaches or fleas in Alaska. We do have swarms of mosquitoes that can truly bring down a moose or caribou. In addition, there is a fly called 'white socks' (because of its clearly white feet) that will literally take a chunk out of any place you might have missed with the bug juice. The white socks' bite makes a mosquito bite seem downright friendly. It lasts for up to two weeks and itches like sin. They love the ankles where the socks slip leaving a little passage to un-doped skin. Itching was an accepted past-time in the camp. We all had ring-around-the-ankle. Our outer clothing was all saturated with bug spray.

Of the camps I set up, this was to be of longer duration and was the nicest of the sites. It sat with three four-man tents, a mess tent complete with refrigerator, freezer, stove, heater, sinks—and a camp cook and helper. There was a shower tent with sinks and a clothes washer, and clothes line. Of course, the beloved outhouse (with camper's art work pictures of fossils) had their proper place.

The camp was situated at the end of the Lime Village Airstrip. A mess tent being right off the end turned out not to be the greatest idea. When one watched a plane come barreling toward the end of the runway it was not a place to loiter.

Stony River braided through the valley and rolling hills around us. The natives of a nearby village were friendly and curious. They had the only telephone, and graciously let me use it. It was in the main house, a small bungalow with vinyl floors. The entire living room floor was covered with mattresses. We had to tune some of our work to their summer schedule because they slept during the day, ate, played volley ball, and then went fishing at night—which was of course Arctic night where the sun gets low, but does not drop below the horizon.

They set up a volley-ball net and there were matches, camp vs natives, most evenings. Chief brought us beautiful king salmon, and several silver salmon for dinner, and we ate well. I think he liked Chris, our camp mainstay, and was looking for a new wife.

Chief asked John and Rick if they were lonely. Maybe there were some women looking for husbands too.

One afternoon we heard a loud buzzing in the air. A neighbor had brought over his ultra-light (flyable tinker-toy plane) and landed to visit after dinner. One of the geologists talked our visitor into letting him fly it. We were pretty sure there would be a death. They really do look like bumbly little super flies. But, after three wild, erratic tries, the geologist landed it in ecstasy over his experience. They are not easy to fly, and the popularity of these fragile planes has waned since those years.

Native women make beautiful birch baskets, all sizes for all uses. The native are proud of their arts, so when we bought things it was for no small price. It was, however, original. They were pleased and shy when we asked them to sign their work.

Maryann, a woman from the village came to work at the camp for 10 to 12 hours a day to keep the camp operable. She was a bouncy, attractive frontier woman, and pastry baker... Yes. She had a dog team she kept for the winter, and we would hear them howl at mealtime.

Maryann brought one of her injured puppies with her to the camp one day. One of the villagers had left to go to McGrath for a three week liquor celebration, and left his dogs to fend for themselves. (It's a different world.) One of the 'left' dogs had attacked Maryann's dog Whiskey, a young, white husky mix.

Our Viet Nam vet helicopter pilot looked at the dog; there is no veterinarian in the village. He asked me to take the dog back with me if it wasn't doing better. I'm a dog lover and agreed, but Whiskey was young and healed amazingly fast with some cleaning, ointment, and rest.

A pilot from McGrath in a plane from Hub Air buzzed our airstrip and barely cleared the trees, making a wide and sudden stop just shy of the main tent, or mess tent. We all went running when we heard the noise. He was also providing some fuel and came to let us know his fuel was perfectly good, not bad as some had claimed. His smarmy behavior wasn't exactly reassuring to the pilot and mechanic.

I flew back to McGrath with him lugging core and rock samples to be transported back to Anchorage, and needing to make a long string of phone calls that I didn't want to rack up on the village phone bill. Our radio and the village phone were not very reliable. Cell phones, had they been available, would have been useless there. No satellite coverage. Those folk in town, paying for this camping trip, wanted our status, and we needed to let our camp provider know we needed supplies and equipment.

On some short survey hops, I was able to tag along in our Aerospatiale A-Star helicopter, a beautiful machine that required a full-time pilot, and a full-time mechanic to do all the maintenance required to keep it in the air and follow regulations.

A summer-hire geologist and I spent most of our time in camp, and we cut slabs of samples and polished them, and changed our clothes a lot with the up-to-the-minute weather.

Dinner was a friendly event with geological camp talk, diversions of the day, and discussions that included fossils called trilobites and three-hole-crinoids. The geologists gave me a couple of lovely fossils. Those hard-shell trilobite creatures were the biggest ever found, measuring three and four inches long.

In the evenings we made occasional trips in the helicopter to do a little fishing, and to drop in on some State folk. The weather had stayed hot and muggy for the better part of the survey, and the white-socks were vicious.

Because it is a rule, any camp generator is always contrary. Nothing makes you want to pick up a hammer like a temperamental generator surging and dying. Our helicopter mechanic would come over and mess with it, and the generator would start its roar again. We all treasured the mechanic. He gained high camp status because he could make anything run.

The camp contractor, John, flew in with special fuel for the helicopter, and lobsters for dinner. He had become a good friend, I always enjoyed seeing him. He did special things on occasion to divert us from routine menus. This trip he brought lobster. Everyone loved him. He also brought care packages from Anchorage.

When I say he flew in, I mean he came in on a Caribou cargo plane with the cargo ramp like I had arrived on. It's a huge, twin engine plane and it was pushing it to land on such a narrow 6,000' strip. We saw them coming, and once again went running away from the strip. But the pilot put the plane between twin trees on each side of the runway, the wings brushed the trees, and he stopped in a blaze of gravel and dust—perfect.

Our San Francisco based geologist brought designer jeans to the geology camp in the middle of Alaska. We were barely aware of designer jeans in Alaska at the time and thought him a dandy. He was. I accidentally got bleach on his pants and he never forgave me. However, I suspect those jeans were prized when he got home with his first-find of their kind fossils, and weathered jeans.

The passion of this trip was fossils from other worlds of times past. In particular, trilobites: *any member of a group of extinct fossil arthropods easily recognized by their distinctive three-lobed, three segmented form*—*exclusively marine animals from about 570 million years ago*—these the first of their kind found in Alaska. The geologists were in search of the Cambrian Period, when trilobites dominated the seas.

Our other favorite fossil was the three holed crinoid: *their distinctive internal skeletons are important Paleozoic index fossil and are known for living in deep water.* This was the first find of crinoid in Alaska as well.

And in no way could we be considered near any deep water in current times. However 500 million years ago, apparently, deep water it was. The thought was awesome. The guys were kind enough to give me several uncommon fossils which I treasure to this day. (I've changed more than the fossils have.)

With daily discoveries, and adventures, camp stories, and comradery, we rarely got to bed before midnight. The guys were always on the helicopter early, and coming back at as late as 7pm.

The volleyball rivalry went on, and the villagers came to get us many evenings to play a few rounds. There was no clear victor, but the players got pretty serious fast.

My office buddy Bill came out to the strip to help me take the core and fossil samples to Minchumina, where we were to be picked up and taken to Anchorage. There were many other better places to fly in and out of, but it was a convenient stop for the morning on a plane headed north. A Twin Otter was supposed to come pick us up, and our load of boxes.

The Minchumina strip was a stand-alone. There was one log to sit on and our plane wasn't there to meet us. There was no radio, just hills, few trees, brush, and wildlife. We stood for a while, sat for a while, walked for a while, and checked our watches and bug dope level frequently.

Like all people standing by an empty airstrip with no facilities and no plane, we wondered if the pilot remembered he was supposed to stop at this strip and pick us up. Did we get dropped off at the wrong place? What bush should we use? As we scoured the skies for signs of our plane we wondered: should we have brought more food and water—a tent, a radio? We had a long while to wonder why we had agreed to this. The sky can look pretty lonesome when there is no plane in sight, and pretty bright when there is.

16.

# Homer Spit General Store

Homer is a beloved *End-of-the-Road* town wrapped around the spectacular Kachemak Bay in middle-south Alaska. The roads to get there were, and in some parts still are, like something out of an old army movie with curves, frost heaves, broken pavement, no road shoulder, and stupid drivers. In Salmon season the road would be packed from Anchorage to Homer. It took one person to drive, and one to watch out for moose, bears, porcupines, rabbits, and race drivers.

When one comes over the hill to Homer, the first thing a person sees is that sweeping bay and the marvel of the peninsula of land jutting into the bay; the Homer Spit. The Spit draws one like a siren. The spit lets a person walk around and experience being in the middle of the Kachemak Bay, Alaska, on dry land. The ocean on all sides.

At the end of the spit there are several landmarks: the Alaska Ferry System, Land's End Resort, the harbor and boat docks, and the Salty Dog Saloon. During the summer the single road is partially lined with little buildings—fish charter businesses, souvenirs, artwork, carving from whale bone and from ivory, jewelry, sweaters, sports gear, pottery, fish floats, and the like. Next door to the Salty Dog sat the Homer Spit General Store. It broke hearts all over the world when the store burned down some years ago. It was irreplaceable.

The General Store would have overlooked the harbor and the Kenai Mountains looking toward Seldovia and the bays—but it was shy on windows. The bay is dotted with halibut, otters, eagles, whales, sea birds, clams, snails, seaweed, and star fish. The ocean smells are heady with marine life. The Homer Spit General Store was a modest, off-kilter, shaggy building with a one-of-a-kind-in-the-world inventory, right there in the middle of the bay.

It sat right next to the tilted Salty Dog Saloon which stands and serves to this day. (A Salty Dog Saloon sweatshirt is a must-buy on one's first trip to Homer.) There was no pavement going on outside or in. I think (it was hard to be sure) that the walls and floor were wood. No space on the wall, shelves, ceiling, staircase/ladder, or attic space was unused. The store also held a little liquor store (closet) and jewelry and tobacco case!

In no way will I ever cover all the things that were hung, propped, snagged, leaned, folded, stacked, or packed in this store. This is from memory, and memories are imperfect, but for fun, I'll try to list many of the items found there.

Shopping was all sidling and walking single file. At first a person could only stand in the door with their mouth open. The mixed smells of oil, tobacco, potatoes, onions, metal, and salt overtook the senses. Then there was a compulsion to buy the kind of rope that might be used on a tanker, or a ship anchor, or a sledge hammer. Where did all this stuff come from?

The cracked glass cash register case inside the door had Timex watches, all kinds of lighters, tobacco tools, flints, fluid, jackknives, gutting knives, sunglasses, gum and candy bars. There was gold nugget jewelry, and small jade and ivory figurines of polar bears, seals, and whales.

Can you imagine inventory lists? Neither could they. I'd bet no one ever knew what all was carried in this store at any one time.

Behind the register and on the walls hung all sorts of batteries, nose spray, cold medicines, aspirin and various pain relievers, jerky, hot shot meat sticks, key rings, condoms, shot glasses, playing cards, dental floss, needles and thread, licorice, finger nail clippers, pens, paper, pencils, and logo tee shirts. There were first aid supplies and canisters, tooth picks, mugs, bowls, Hershey bars, clocks, bumper stickers, glues, chap-sticks, and ear plugs, feminine hygiene, birth control, and medical supplies.

One can only wonder what washed over the side of the boats, or got lost in the general chaos of fishing boat cabins. They are not known for their tidiness. Who can live without chap-stick, or Elmer's, Jack Daniels, or superglue? Or duct tape! Let alone oranges.

On the one main wall hung lanterns, wicks, candles, post cards, wooden 'joke' cards, *land's end* souvenirs, fly swatters, and magazines.

On the shelves were mac and cheese, canned chili, Spam, coffee, peanut butter, jelly, corn beef hash, spaghetti, Campbell's soup, tuna, sardines, mustard, ketchup, mayo, tinned sausages, green beans, pork and beans—what have I missed? Honey, sugar, salt, and pepper—and Tabasco sauce.

More scabby looking shelves held Sailor crackers, potato chips, and corn nuts. There were home-style body regulators such as prunes, raisins, laxatives, anti-diarrhea pills, antacids, and lemons.

And still more stuff crammed in every space including can openers, Crisco, instant coffee, Folger's coffee in a can, tea, noodles, Vaseline, salt and pepper, tea, Tang, marshmallows, Lifesavers, Tums, cocoa, mints, pickles, applesauce, canned carrots, tin foil, wax paper, clear wrap, and baggies.

On the floor, baskets of potatoes, garlic, cabbage, and onions sat alongside waders, come-alongs, axes, pliers, and things I'm sure I don't know what they are for. A tiny paperback book stand took up little space with maximum selection.

From the freezer was Janet Lee Ice Cream, ice cream bars, frozen dinners, and herring bait, hamburger, steaks, pot pies, cool whip, and frozen orange juice.

In the cooler was milk, cream, various cheeses, butter or margarine, and Pillsbury biscuits.

Nearby there were small baskets with some tough looking fruit such as apples, oranges, lemons, and bananas—and vegies: carrots, celery, and whatever was in season.

From the ceiling hung buckets, red peppers, anchors, marine equipment, grappling hooks, more potatoes, cord, cable, rigging, pipes, line, and toilet insides.

On the back wall were shelves and hooks for shampoo, dish soap, bar soap, bleach, ammonia, and laundry soap. To the right were marine chemicals, marine toilet paper, flashlights, commercial and pleasure fishing lures, fishing poles, fishing rods, fishing line, fishing leaders, fishing baskets, and fishing nets.

The hard-core area by the stairs (it was closer to a ladder) held (one way or another) anchors, engine oil, WD-40, chain, rope, caulking, plumbing supplies, hammers, screwdrivers, fish floats, thing-a-ma-bobs, life vests, paper products, paddles, crab pots, light bulbs, duct tape, fuses, screws, nails, tacks, hooks, and more.

The attic held the best long underwear and gloves and tin dishes and cook wear a person could ever hope to find. It had baking pans, flatware, cooking pots, head scarves, fishing gloves of all description, all piled or hung around on driftwood shelves and saw horses topped with plywood. There were sleeping bags, hats, fishing nets, rain gear, pancake turners, cutting boards, wool socks, underwear, tee shirts, safety pins, sweaters and sweatshirts, dishtowels, overalls, mugs, backpacks, suspenders, rubber boots, blankets, sheets, and chop sticks.

It was impossible to walk out without buying something—even when one was on a tight budget. The senses were overwhelmed, the clerks disinterested, the sailors wandered in and out on the way to the Salty Dog, the private drinkers wandering in and out, and then there were we happy visitors.

It's a terrible thing to have lost places such as these general stores. Homer still has an ACE hardware store that gives some organized competition to the old general store. But they have computers. Back then, it was an art to stock the space, have a feel for what people might need, and know where every item was.

I still miss that curiosity-shop of a general store. The art is all but lost.

PS: I recently saw a travel special on Homer and the end of the road. It was portrayed as distant, primitive, rustic, dangerous, and threatening. Homer is about as threatening as a sled dog. It has one of the mildest climates in the state. There is two to four lane highway from Anchorage to Homer, and it's about a four hour drive past many towns and villages and some Russian architecture. I can't imagine what that travel reporter was smoking. Everybody loves Homer and the End of The Road.

In conclusion, Alaska has been one continuing adventure over these years. There's the grittier combat fishing and camping on the Russian, Anchor, and Kenai Rivers. Over the years workmates and friends favored fly-in fishing trips down south, and boat trips out of Seward and Homer.

I've had the opportunity to spend time in Kotzebue, the Arctic National Wildlife Refuge, and the Alaska Peninsula. I'd love to revisit all three but the chances are low. I've been shipboard and waded in the Arctic Ocean, and the Beaufort Sea. Much of this is thanks to work opportunities and kind friends.

Now my Alaska adventures are generally in an Alaska-proof well-traveled motorhome with my husband Dick, and our dog Rose. We have a growing fondness now for fossil hunting. But who knows what may come next?

Many of you have noteworthy travel experiences that surpass mine. I encourage you to make a list of your personal adventures and travel – you will see your life through new eyes.

www.ingramcontent.com/pod-product-compliance
Lightning Source LLC
Chambersburg PA
CBHW060834050426
42453CB00008B/689